# Abundance

## 100+ PLANT-BASED RECIPES TO SAVOUR YEAR ROUND

## ANNA VALENTINE

# Contents

# Introduction

*Abundance* is the culmination of the best of the best of my seasonal recipes enhanced with everyday plant-based essentials made from scratch with whole foods. Inspired by the plant kingdom's abundance, the recipes you will find in this book are what I feed my family every day. I strive to make plant-based food accessible, easy, healthy and delicious. Recipes that you will come back to time and time again.

This is a compendium of plant-based recipes, the everyday basics that are my fridge and pantry staples which I literally make every week. If you are vegetarian, vegan, plant predominant or just keen to eat more plants, you have come to the right place. I have even gone so far as making plant-protein meat alternatives out of natural ingredients without any unnecessary additives and preservatives. Super tasty, these hit the spot for smoky cravings, and are there for you if you just want to give the kids burgers or nuggets and chips for dinner. The options for making plant milk, cheese, butter, cream, amongst others are there if you want them, and every recipe can be made fully plant-based and gluten-free.

Eating with the seasons ensures you are getting optimal nutrition, as nutrients are at their highest in foods harvested when they are ripe – it is also far more cost effective. Eat a rainbow every day is my mantra and within these pages are a plethora of vegetable dishes of every colour that will make your mouth water and your tummy happy, all nutritionally balanced, healthy, and inspired by food from all over the world.

Every meal of the day is taken care of, from breakfast and brunch dishes to sweet baking and desserts, plus an extensive salads and soups section. Whether you are after a quick and easy bread recipe or a meal to share with family and friends, the light meals and mains sections have the full range of fresh vibrant summertime fare to cosy winter comfort foods and everything in between.

# My Plant-Based Pantry

### Acidophilus yogurt
A probiotic strain of bacteria which creates a tangy flavour, the presence of lactic acid will curdle milk.

### Activated charcoal
Most edible versions are made from burnt coconut shells. It binds to toxins drawing them out of the body. It is often used for its black colouring in foods.

### Agar powder
Made from a red seaweed it is used for gelling, thickening, stabilising and emulsifying.

### Agave syrup
Syrup extracted from the core of the agave plant.

### Aquafaba
The cooking liquid from tinned beans or legumes which has a thick, viscous consistency.

### Banana blossom
The unpollenated end of the banana flower once the bunch has set, also known as the banana heart.

### Buckwheat flour
A flowering plant with edible grain-like seeds. A pseudo grain, which is a type of grain that doesn't grow on grasses but is used similarly to other cereals, nutrient dense and gluten free.

### Cacao powder
Cold pressed, unroasted cacao beans ground into a powder.

### Chia seeds
Powerhouse of nutrients, with high absorption qualities can be used as an egg substitute or for thickening.

### Coconut aminos
Fermented coconut palm nectar used in place of soy sauce or tamari.

### Coconut nectar
Nectar extracted from the coconut flower.

### Cream of tartar
An acid similar to lemon or vinegar, potassium hydrogen tartrate is a byproduct of winemaking which is used to stabilise.

### Dried seaweed
Marine algae that grow along seashores, generally anchored to the sea bottom or rocks. The most common for culinary use are kombu, kelp, nori (karengo), wakame, sea lettuce.

### Edible weeds
Non cultivated edible wild plants, examples are onion weed, dandelion, nasturtium, plantain, nettle, chickweed.

### Extra-virgin olive oil
Made from the first pressing of the olives so is the least processed and contains the highest amount of nutrients.

### Flaxseeds
Also known as linseeds these seeds have very similar qualities to chia seeds but need to be ground first for best results.

### Guar gum
Used as a thickener in liquids or as a binder for gluten-free baking, helps prevent crumbling and falling apart.

### Hemp hearts
The inner nutrient-dense part of the hemp seed.

### Himalayan pink salt
A rich mineral salt from the Punjab region in Pakistan.

## Kasha/groats

Toasted buckwheat groats. Groats are the unhulled kernals of various whole grains and pseudo grains that include the cereal germ and fiber-rich bran portion of the grain, as well as the endosperm.

## Kraut juice

The liquid from making saurekraut or the like. It has a sour, tangy flavour and contains lactic acid, probiotics and can aid fermentation if active.

## Maca powder

A cruciferous vegetable otherwise known as Peruvian ginseng. Used in herbalism and general wellness as a supplement and body support.

## Medjool dates

Softer than other varieties, they easily blend into recipes with no need to soak beforehand.

## Nutritional yeast

An inactive form of yeast which has a cheesy umami flavour is naturally high in B vitamins, proteins and essential amino acids.

## Passata

Uncooked, crushed tomato puree.

## Psyllium husk

The husk from plantago flowers commonly known as plantain, it needs to be activated with warm liquid to create its glutinous gel-type consistancy before adding to recipes.

## Quinoa

A flowering plant grown for its edible and highly nutrious seeds, is naturally gluten free, also known as a pseudo grain.

## Smoke liquid

Made by condensing smoke from burning wood it is used to give a smoky barbeque flavour to foods.

## Sorghum flour

A nutrient-rich gluten-free cereal grain from a flowering grass.

## Spelt flour

Ancient wheat grain, also known as dinkel it is naturally low in gluten, easier to digest than modern wheat and is high in fiber.

## Tahini

Ground sesame seed paste.

## Tamarind paste

A sour fruit that grows in pods which is like a sour date with many fiberous parts that need to be removed before palatable.

## Tempeh

Fermented whole soybeans which have been naturally cultured, it has a firm texture and umami flavour.

## Tofu

Soy milk coagulated with nigari, gypsom or an acid such as vinegar to form curds and whey, the curds are then pressed into a cake of varying firmness with a sponge-like texture to soft curds.

## Wheat gluten

A natural protein that acts like a binder, holding food together and adding a stretchy, chewy quality.

## Yogurt starter culture (vegan)

Live probiotic bacteria and yeasts.

PLANT MILK
MASH CRACKERS
PLANT BUTTER
VEGGIE MITE
PLANT CHEESE
ALMOND RICOTTA
CASHEW CHEESE
DAIRY RICOTTA
HEMP PARMESAN
MACADAMIA OR CASHEW CREAM
CASHEW SOUR CREAM
EGG SUBSTITUTES
PLANT PROTEIN 'MEATS'
SMOKY SUBSTITUTES
HUMMUS WITH CHICKPEAS & ROAST OLIVES
KALE CHIPS
YOGHURT
PESTO
BALSAMIC REDUCTION
MAYONNAISE
JAM JAR DRESSINGS
VEGGIE STOCK

# Everyday Basics

# Plant Milk

One of my top priorities for a plant milk was that it held up to the coffee test, and this absolutely does, however, you do need to have both the liquids at the same temperature for this to be successful. You don't want to heat the milk over 60 degrees. My go-to combo is either oat, macadamia or cashew for their creaminess, almonds for calcium and hemp hearts for magnesium which helps your body absorb calcium. I utilise a nutribullet to make my plant milk, but any high-speed blender will do. The solids ratio when making your own milk means you don't need to add thickeners or stabilisers to your milk to make it creamy. It lasts in a sterilised jar in the fridge for a week.

*Vegan | Gluten free*
*Makes 700ml*

1 cup hemp hearts, almonds, macadamia, oats or cashew nuts
650ml hottest tap water
a pinch of salt
1 tablespoon maple syrup or 1 medjool date (optional)

Measure the oats, macadamia or cashews, almonds, hemp hearts, water, maple syrup and salt into a food processor. Secure the lid and blitz for 1 minute.

Leave to cool for about 1 hour, then blitz again for 1 minute. Pour through a nut milk bag, or similar, placed on a sieve over a jug and squeeze well to remove all the liquid, pour into a sterilised jar, cap and keep in the fridge.

Shake well before use.

# Mash Crackers

These crunchy light moreish crackers are the perfect way to use up the almond pulp from making the Almond Ricotta or Plant Milk. I recommend freezing the pulp from the milk until you have two cups worth, as it goes off in the fridge quite quickly (see picture on p15).

*Vegan | Gluten free*
*Makes 30*

1/2 cup flaxseeds
1/2 cup water
1/2 cup psyllium
3/4 cup hot water
2 cups almond or nut milk pulp
1 sprig rosemary, leaves finely chopped
3 tablespoons nutritional yeast
1 tsp salt
1/4 tsp pepper
1 tablespoon extra-virgin olive oil
1/2 tsp flaky sea salt or Himalayan pink salt

Mix the flaxseeds with the first measurement of water. Leave to absorb for 20 minutes, stirring once during this time.

Preheat the oven to 150°C. Measure the psyllium husk and hot water into a mixing bowl and stir together. Add the nut pulp, rosemary, nutritional yeast, salt and pepper. Mix to combine. Add the flaxseed mixture and stir through.

Line two trays with baking paper and grease with olive oil. Place half the mixture on each tray. Evenly flatten out the mix (with greased hands is easiest), then cover with another piece of baking paper. Using a rolling pin, roll out as flat and evenly as you can. Sprinkle salt over the top of each and bake for 25 minutes.

Remove from the oven and, using another tray or board covered with baking paper, flip the cracker over and peel off the baking paper. Cut into desired shapes and place back in the oven for a further 35–40 minutes, until dried out and crispy. Cool and store in an airtight container or tin.

Plant Milk

# Plant Butter

*This butter is semi soft straight from the fridge, is perfect for toast and even melts nicely in the pan at a medium heat for frying. I utilise the mini food processor as the higher speed and power is better for this job. I like to add the shea butter as an extra creamy element and it melts less readily than coconut oil, and hemp hearts for their creaminess as well as nutrition. I add the flaxseed and guar gum to emulsify, turmeric for colour as well as nutritional yeast which, along with the apple cider vinegar, gives it a little cultured tang.*

## Vegan | Gluten free
## Makes 2 1/2 cups

1 cup hemp hearts
1 cup coconut oil (refined, if you don't want it to taste of coconut), firm
1/2 cup shea butter (or extra coconut oil)
2 tablespoons extra-virgin olive oil
2 tablespoons ground flaxseeds (optional)
3 tablespoons nutritional yeast
2 tsp salt
1/4 tsp ground turmeric
2 tsp apple cider vinegar
1/2 tsp guar gum

Measure the hemp hearts into the food processor. Blitz until a butter forms, you may need to scrape down the sides a couple of times.

Add the coconut oil, shea butter, extra-virgin olive oil, flaxseeds (if using), nutritional yeast, salt, turmeric, apple cider vinegar and guar gum. Blitz until combined. (Don't leave it running too long or the oils will get too hot, melt and separate.)

Transfer to a lidded container and store in the fridge.

# Veggie Mite

*I created this healthy, refined, sugar-free version of the well-known spread as I literally have Marmite and hempseed oil on my toast every day and wanted to recreate it so they were combined and I just have to spread one on there! Sesame seeds are packed with calcium and zinc, molasses is also high in calcium as well as iron, selenium and copper. You could also buy black tahini and just stir the other ingredients thoroughly, if doing this you possibly won't need the water.*

## Vegan | Gluten free
## Makes 300g

1/2 cup hulled sesame seeds
1/2 cup black sesame seeds
3 tablespoons hemp seed oil
1 tsp salt
2–3 tablespoons blackstrap molasses or other liquid sweetener
2 tablespoons miso paste
1 tablespoon nutritional yeast
1 tsp activated charcoal
1 tsp kelp powder
2 tablespoons water

Preheat the oven to 180°C. Measure the sesame seeds into a roasting tray and bake for 5–8 minutes until the white sesame seeds release their oils.

Remove from the oven and transfer to a food processor and add the hempseed oil and salt. Blitz until a paste has formed, this takes a while (10 minutes or so) and you will need to scrape down the edges a few times.

Add the blackstrap molasses, miso paste, nutritional yeast, activated charcoal, kelp powder and water and blitz well until smooth. Transfer to a jar.

# Plant Cheese

*I have tried many plant-based cheeses in my time and it is definitely one of those foods that no one wants to miss out on and also has a few qualities it must fulfil. The versatility of cheese is one of these, it must taste cheesy, slice easily, be able to be grated and melt. This cheese does it all! I am super pleased with it and I hope you will be too. If you cook the cheese for longer it gets more of a 'cheddar' flavour and texture, it does tend to separate if cooked too long, don't worry though I think it gives it more character.*

## Vegan | Gluten free
### Makes 1 x 14cm wide, 5cm deep bowl-shaped cheese

350ml plant milk
1/4 cup nutritional yeast
1/4 cup refined coconut oil
15g strong agar powder
1 tablespoon tapioca or potato flour
1 tablespoon pea flour
1/8 tsp ground turmeric
1/4 tsp smoked paprika (optional)
1 tsp salt
1 clove garlic, peeled but kept whole or 1 tsp garlic or onion powder
2 tablespoons apple cider vinegar or kraut juice

Grease the bowl or container. Measure the milk, nutritional yeast, coconut oil, agar powder, tapioca flour, pea flour, turmeric, smoked paprika (if using), salt and garlic into a pot. Whisk on a medium heat until it comes to the boil. Turn down to a simmer and add the vinegar, whisk in and cook for 1 minute for a mild cheese and 5 minutes for cheddar.

Remove from the heat, remove the garlic clove, and transfer to the prepared bowl or container. Cool then refrigerate, uncovered, until completely cold. Cover the container with a plate and tip upside down, give it a little tap to help it slip out. Slice and enjoy.

Store in an airtight container in the fridge.

*Plant Cheese with Mash Crackers*

# Almond Ricotta

This delicate ricotta has a lovely taste and texture. The almonds benefit from a long soak which make the skins easy to remove or just leave the skins on, it doesn't affect the finished cheese and is purely aesthetic. It is essential to heat and stir slowly and gently, 90 degrees is just below boiling point, don't try and rush it. If you don't have a thermometer, you can tell it's coming to the boil by bubbles forming at the sides of the pot. Don't jump the gun though – give them a gentle stir and if they form again immediately then you are good to go. The little ricotta baskets are quite hard to come by but you can make your own by drilling holes in a container or using the inner from a small salad spinner.

*Vegan | Gluten free*
*Makes 1 x 400g cheese*

**2 cups almonds, soaked for 24 hours with cold water or 2 hours with hot water**
**4 cups water**
**a pinch of salt**
**2 tablespoons apple cider vinegar**
**2 pieces of lemon peel**

Soak the almonds by covering completely with water. Once soaked, drain the water and remove the skins. Blend almonds with the fresh water and salt.

Place a sieve over a pot with a nut bag or very fine muslin and pour the mix through. Squeeze out as much liquid as you can and set the pulp aside.

Heat the milk very gently on a low heat. Stir very gently at 3-minute intervals until it reaches 90°C, about 15–20 minutes. Remove from the heat and add the vinegar and lemon peel, stir gently and leave to cool, undisturbed.

Remove peel and pour through sterilised muslin. Leave to drain for 11/2 hours. Transfer to a mould, then drain overnight in the fridge. Gently tip out of the mould and enjoy.

Store in the fridge in a lidded container.

# Cashew Cheese

Perfect for a plant-based cheese board or antipasto platter this cheese is soft and spreadable, packed with protein, vitamin B12 and totally delicious. It gets its cheesiness and vitamin B12 from the nutritional yeast. Cashew nuts are nutrient-dense and linked to many positive health benefits. This cheese is easy to whip up and will store in the fridge for a good week. You will need a cheese cloth, muslin or the like to form the cheese ball. To sterilise the cloth, add to a pot, cover it in boiling water and boil for five minutes. Drain, leave to cool a moment before touching it, then drape it over the sieve ready to use. Choose your preferred herbs for coating the cheese. I have given a few suggestions, but mix and match to your taste.

## Vegan | Gluten free
## Makes 1 x 500g cheese

2 cups raw cashews
1 litre water
2 cloves garlic, peeled
zest and juice of 2 lemons
2 tablespoons extra-virgin olive oil
1/4 cup nutritional yeast flakes
1 tsp salt
1/4 tsp cracked black pepper
1 tablespoon sweet smoked paprika (for smoky version)
2 tsp smoke liquid (for smoky version)

### For herb coating:
1/2 cup dried herbs, parsley, dill, chives or onion weed, coriander, thyme, oregano or rosemary
1/2 tsp flaked sea salt
1/4 tsp cracked black pepper

### For smoky coating:
2 tsp cracked black pepper
1 tsp smoked paprika (sweet or hot)

Soak the cashews in water – 4 hours in cold water or 1 hour in hot water.

Drain and add to a food processor along with the garlic, lemon, olive oil, yeast flakes, salt and pepper. Add the smoky elements if needed.

Process ingredients together to form a smooth paste – you will need to scrape the processor a couple of times to incorporate all evenly.

Place the sterilised cloth at the bottom of a sieve placed over a bowl.

Scoop the mixture out of the processor into the cloth and gather up the edges and twist gently to form a disk shape.

Secure with a rubber band and place in the fridge to set for 12-24 hours.  Not a lot (if any) liquid will come out, but the dry cold of the fridge takes any excess moisture away.

Prepare the coating and place onto a plate.

Take the cheese from the fridge and remove the cheese cloth carefully. Undo the rubber band, open out the cloth and tip the cheese disk straight onto the coating. Then remove the rest of the cloth, using a spatula to flip the cheese over and gently pat the herbs over the rest of the cheese.

Return to the fridge uncovered for another 24-48 hours. This will dry the cheese further and create a 'rind' – the longer you leave it the firmer the rind will be. It is now ready to serve. Store uncovered in the fridge for a week or so. The cheese ages as it sits in the drying air of the fridge, if you cover it, it will sweat and potentially mould.

# Dairy Ricotta

I like to refer to this as easy cheese, because it really is so easy and quick to make. Similar to paneer, it can also be fried like haloumi, stirred through pasta, covered in herbs and baked, or used in sweeter options like cheesecake fillings or tarts.

You will need:

- a small plastic or metal container with many draining holes, a ricotta mould, the basket out of fresh mozzarella from the supermarket or a sieve lined with muslin or similar (sterilised in boiling water first).

- I also like to have jars ready and waiting for the whey so it seals with the heat.

- a slotted spoon to take the curds from the whey.

- a plastic scraper to stir the milk and to get the last of the curds out of the pan.

You will also need to set up the sieve on top of a large jug or bowl and have the mould sitting on a container to raise it out of the bowl it is sitting in so the whey drains immediately. Ensure that all the equipment is rinsed with hottest tap water and that jars are air dried, or oven dried at 150°C for 5 minutes.

If you use yoghurt as the starter, it will take slightly longer to form the curds and you get a milkier whey.

Vinegar (my preference) forms the curds quickly and gives a firmer finished product, which is good for frying. I don't salt my ricotta so it can be used for sweet or savoury dishes but you absolutely can – do this while heating the milk.

## Gluten free
## Makes 1 x 400g cheese

**2 litres dairy milk, full fat, farmhouse or raw**
**1/3 cup white vinegar or lemon juice**
**or 1 cup plain natural acidophilus yoghurt**

Pour the milk into a heavy-based pot and gently heat on a medium temperature stirring often until it reaches 80-90°C. This will take approximately 10 minutes.

Remove from heat, add the vinegar or lemon juice or yoghurt and stir in gently and slowly.

Stop stirring once the curds have formed and scoop them out into the basket sitting in the bowl.

Tip off the excess whey from the bowl and discard.

Cool the curds in the fridge for two hours. Check on the curds after half an hour to remove any further whey that has accumulated.

Meanwhile jar up the hot whey. The whey can be used in place of water or stock in recipes such as risotto, bread making or cheese sauces.

Once the curds are cold tip the cheese carefully out of the basket onto a plate. Then return to the fridge uncovered overnight. Store covered in the fridge for up to a week.

# Hemp Parmesan

*This hemp parmesan has become a staple in the fridge here at The Veggie Tree; we all love it! Savoury, salty, creamy and packed with nutrition, it is the perfect topper for everything from pasta to risotto, pesto to fritters, basically anything you would usually add parmesan to. It doesn't melt but parmesan isn't really a melty cheese anyway. This hemp parmesan gives anything you add it to a delicious savoury creamy cheesy flavour which you will be addicted to in no time.*

*Vegan | Gluten free*

*Makes 1 cup*

**1 clove garlic, peeled or 1 tsp garlic powder**
**1/3 cup hemp hearts**
**1/3 cup macadamia or cashew nuts**
**1/3 cup nutritional yeast**
**1 tsp salt**

Place the garlic, hemp hearts, macadamia or cashew nuts, nutritional yeast and salt into a food processor. Pulse until finely chopped.

Store in the fridge in a sealed jar (if you used fresh garlic) otherwise can be stored in the pantry.

# Macadamia or Cashew Cream

This quick, easy cream is a cinch to make. It's creamy, delicious and you can sub it into any recipe that calls for single cream. In saying this, as it is more of a single cream, it doesn't whip, so if you need this quality use chilled coconut cream. If I am adding this cream to a creamy mushroom sauce, for example, I won't bother straining it as the solids are minimal.

## Vegan | Gluten free
### Makes 2 cups

1 cup raw cashew nuts
2 cups hot water
1 1/4 cup water

Cover the cashew nuts with the hot water and leave for 1 hour, or use cold water and soak for 3–4 hours to soften.

Drain the water off, rinse the nuts and place in a high-speed blender along with the fresh water. Blitz together well, strain through a nut milk bag for a smoother cream.

Store in the fridge for up to a week.

# Cashew Sour Cream

This tangy, creamy, probiotic sour cream is a staple in our fridge. We enjoy it on all sorts including nachos, tacos, wraps, baked potatoes, on top of soups and as a dip. It thickens in the fridge and I will often leave it out for 24 hours with a muslin or similar over the top to start the fermentation which gives it an extra tang and flavour. It keeps in the fridge for a couple of weeks in a clean, sterilised jar.

## Vegan | Gluten free
### Makes 450 ml

1 cup cashew nuts, soaked 1 hour in boiling water
150ml water
zest and juice of 1 lemon
2–3 tablespoons apple cider vinegar
1/2 tsp salt

Measure the cashew nuts, water, lemon zest and juice, apple cider vinegar and salt into a high-speed blender and blitz until very smooth. Check for acidity and add the extra measurement of vinegar if needed.

Store in the fridge.

Cashew Sour Cream

# Egg Substitutes

## Aquafaba (white bean or legume cooking liquid)

**3 tablespoons of aquafaba liquid per egg, 2 tablespoons for white, 1 tablespoon for yolk.**

This is a fabulous substitute for getting air into plant-based cooking. However, it doesn't stand up to high cooking temperatures very well. For fluffing up, 1/4 tsp of cream of tartar per 2 tablespoons of aquafaba is added to help hold its volume.

## Chia seeds

**One tablespoon of chia seeds with four tablespoons of water and left to absorb for 10 minutes minimum, replaces one egg.**

Chia seeds are most commonly used for smoothie-type liquids for making into chia pudding. I like to use it in baking also, but you will always need more raising agents such as baking powder to achieve the rise required.

## Applesauce

**1/4 cup unsweetened applesauce per egg**

Applesauce adds moisture to baking. Fruit purée does tend to make the final product denser so the addition of an extra teaspoon of baking powder helps.

## Tofu

**1/4 cup tofu per egg**

Most commonly used in savoury baked goods such as quiches, tarts or cheesecakes when you want the final product to be quite dense.

## Banana

**1/4 cup mashed banana per egg**

Generally it is 1 regular-sized banana per egg. Banana egg replacement is mostly used in baking – be mindful of the flavour profiles. Fruit purée does tend to make the final product denser, so the addition of an extra teaspoon of baking powder helps.

## Flaxseed, ground

**One tablespoon of ground flaxseed to two tablespoons of water and left to absorb for 10 minutes minimum, replaces one egg.**

You can also use whole flaxseeds with the same ratio as the chia seeds. I like to use flax eggs for savoury dishes such as patties, sausages, crackers and pasta as it is a great binder.

# Plant protein 'meats'

I really wanted to create some plant-based proteins from scratch so that you can make your own alternatives which aren't full of ingredients you don't recognise. There are many highly processed plant-based alternative meats out there, some made of 'real' food and some not. It is better to keep processed foods to a minimum but that doesn't mean you have to live off rice and beans all the time. I love to be able to make my own proteins that are similar to meat products. It gives you a different texture and means you are not missing out on the hero proteins all the time.

# Wheat meat | Seitan

I love the versatility of this recipe; it has a chewy texture and meaty 'mouth feel'. You can flavour it with an array of flavourings and how cool is it to be able to make meat from flour! Kneading this wheat meat for longer creates a chewier texture and I always utilise the stock it has simmered in for gravy or a sauce with the meal.

Flavouring herbs and spice combinations:

Chicken – thyme, rosemary, parsley, dried ground coriander
Beef – black pepper, ground cumin, mustard, oregano, rosemary
Pork – smoked paprika, liquid smoke, sage, marjoram

## Vegan
## Makes 600g

**1 1/2 cup wheat gluten**
**2 tsp vegetable bouillon**
**2 tablespoons flavouring herbs and spices (see above)**
**1 clove garlic, crushed or 1 tsp garlic powder**
**2 tablespoons light soy sauce, tamari or coconut aminos**
**2 tablespoons apple cider vinegar**
**2 tablespoons extra-virgin olive oil or refined coconut oil, melted**
**1 tsp salt**
**1/2 tsp cracked black pepper**
**1 cup water**

### Simmer Stock

**1 litre vegetable stock**
**or**
**1 litre water**
**2 tsp vegetable bouillon powder**
**3 bay leaves**

Place all ingredients, apart from the Simmer Stock (liquid vegetable stock) in a mixing bowl. Using a dough hook or butter knife, mix together until it forms one mass then kneed for 5 minutes. Leave to rest for 5 minutes.

Meanwhile, bring the simmer stock to the boil. Remove the dough from the bowl and cut into four pieces. Place into the broth and simmer with the lid on for 30 minutes. Remove from the broth and cool.

### Wheat Meat Pieces

Instead of creating one mass with the dough, just leave it in irregular pieces and pop them into the simmering broth.

### Wheat Meat Patties

Slice into 5mm thick and 8cm rounds, about palm sized, before simmering. They will enlarge while cooking,

### Pulled Wheat Meat

When it is cool enough to touch, using a fork, tear it into bite-sized pieces.

# Smoky Substitutes

*One of my favourite flavour profiles is smoky, and the food that so many people eating plant-based diets miss is bacon. So I like to have a few alternatives in my back pocket for satisfying this craving. Marinating for a few hours enhances the depth of flavour, especially for the tofu and mushrooms, but is not essential.*

Vegan | Gluten free
Serves 4

2–3 tablespoons light soy sauce, tamari or coconut aminos
2–3 tablespoons oil, extra-virgin olive or hemp seed
1 tablespoon liquid smoke
1 tablespoon maple syrup
1 tablespoon smoked paprika
1 tsp garlic powder or 1 clove garlic, crushed
1/2 tsp Himalayan or flaked salt
300g firm tofu, sliced width-ways into 12 x 5mm slices or 300g tempeh, sliced width-ways into 18 x 5mm slices or 300g mushrooms, cut into 5mm slices
2 tablespoons coconut oil, virgin or refined, melted

Place the soy sauce, oil, liquid smoke, maple syrup, smoked paprika, garlic and salt in a flat container or bowl. Stir together then add the tofu, tempeh or mushrooms and mix carefully to coat all the pieces. Leave to marinate, if time allows, flipping once during this time.

Preheat the oven to 150°C and line a tray with baking paper. Place each slice onto the paper (with as much marinade stuck to it as possible) with 1cm space between each and bake for 25 minutes.

Remove from the oven. Drizzle with 1 tablespoon of coconut oil, flip over, brush any remaining marinade over the top of each slice, drizzle with the other tablespoon of coconut oil and return to the oven for 25 minutes.

Remove from the oven, slice or add whole slices to BLTs, wraps, pasta dishes, into pies and quiches or serve with a cooked breakfast.

Keep in a covered container in the fridge. Use plenty of oil and a low heat to warm, if needed.

# Hummus with Crispy Chickpeas and Roasted Olives

*Hummus is the mother of all dips. It's protein-packed with chickpeas and tahini, is super easy to make and really is better than bought stuff. Dressing it up with dukkah, roasted olives and extra-virgin olive oil adds texture and boosts flavours, but these aren't essential. Also, a little tip, if you are cooking the chickpeas from scratch, add half a teaspoon of baking soda to the cooking water which softens the shells of the chickpeas, this makes for a smoother silkier hummus. I always cook, then cool the chickpeas in the water I've cooked them in and store them like this. If not making the hummus straight away, this ensures the chickpeas stay soft. Warm hummus is absolutely delicious and if you make it warm it tends to turn out ultra silky.*

## Vegan | Gluten free
## Makes 400g | 2 cups

400g can chickpeas, drained, reserve 2 tablespoons aquafaba (brine) or 1/2 cup dried chickpeas (see method for cooking instructions)
1–2 cloves garlic, peeled
1/4 cup tahini
2 tablespoons extra-virgin olive oil
zest and juice of 1 lemon
1 tsp salt
cracked black pepper, to taste

## Crispy Chickpeas

400g can chickpeas, drained
2 tablespoons extra-virgin olive oil
1 tsp flaked salt
1/4 tsp cracked black pepper

## Roasted Olives

200g olives
1 tablespoon extra-virgin olive oil
zest of 1 orange
1 tablespoon fennel or cumin seeds
a pinch of salt
a pinch of pepper

If cooking your own chickpeas, soak the dried chickpeas in 2 cups water for 6 hours or overnight, drain water. Place the chickpeas in a pot and cover with 3 cups (750ml) of fresh water, bring to the boil and simmer until soft, about 40 minutes, the chickpeas should squash easily between your fingers when ready.

Measure the chickpeas, garlic, tahini, olive oil, lemon, salt and pepper into a food processor. Blitz the ingredients together for a minute, then add 2 tablespoons of aquafaba and blitz for 5 minutes until a silky smooth consistency is reached. Top with extra-virgin olive oil, Crispy Chickpeas and Roasted Olives.

To make the Crispy Chickpeas, preheat the oven to 200°C. Measure the chickpeas, olive oil, salt and pepper into a roasting pan and roast for 20 minutes, stirring a couple of times during cooking. Remove when crispy and serve on top of the hummus.

To make the Roasted Olives, preheat the oven to 200°C. Measure the olives, olive oil, orange zest, fennel or cumin seeds, salt and pepper into a roasting pan and roast for 10 minutes, stirring once during cooking. Remove from the oven and serve on top of the hummus.

# Kale Chips

*This is a pretty flexible recipe; you can really use any amount of curly kale, cavolo nero, silverbeet or even beetroot leaves. You can have the oven slightly hotter if you're in a hurry, but long and slow is best. You will need your biggest, flattest oven trays. Line them with baking paper. To strip the leaves off the kale, pull your fingers up either side of the stem from the base, don't worry if they are a little uneven, I like to leave mine as is, but you can tear the leaves into pieces too.*

*Vegan | Gluten free*
*Makes 8 cups*

**8 cups kale, stems removed and torn into pieces, if preferred**
**2–3 tablespoons extra-virgin olive oil**
**1 clove garlic, crushed**
**3 tablespoons nutritional savoury yeast flakes**
**1/2 tsp flaked sea salt or Himalayan pink salt**

Preheat the oven to 80°C. Put the leaves into a large bowl and drizzle with the olive oil. Add the garlic and massage through, rubbing the leaves well so they have a slight coating.

Arrange them on baking trays in a single layer and top with the savoury yeast flakes and salt. Cook for about 30 minutes. They're ready when completely dried out and very brittle.

Transfer to a jar to store, they will last one month this way, as long as the lid is replaced straight after any chips are removed.

# Yoghurt

Creamy, tangy, smooth and delicious this homemade yoghurt recipe really hits the spot for those who aren't so keen on coconut yogurts but want a plant-based option (although you can absolutely use coconut cream in the recipe).

Because of the microbiology of yogurt making, we must be mindful of what we are feeding the milk to make the yoghurt set. I like to use a plant-based cream for yoghurt so it's thick and creamy. Plant-sourced cream does not contain lactose, so you need to introduce sugars and proteins to feed the bacteria. The bacteria still produce some acid in dairy-free cream, so the flavour is slightly tart. However, plant-based milk does not have the same proteins as dairy milk that coagulate in the presence of an acid, so you need to add a thickener to make it thick and creamy, especially if you aren't using coconut cream.

Agar powder is the perfect plant-based thickener, a seaweed extract which is readily available from the supermarket.

## Plant-based yogurt
### Makes 600ml

**600ml full-fat plant cream (cashew cream page 24)**
**1/2 tsp Agar powder**
**1 tablespoon lemon juice**
**1 tablespoon maple syrup or sugar**
**1-2 tablespoons already made plant-based yogurt or**
**1/8 tsp vegan yogurt starter culture**

Pour the milk/cream into a saucepan, sprinkle in the agar powder and warm to 75°C, stirring constantly. Meanwhile, whisk together the lemon juice, maple syrup and plant-based yoghurt (if using).

Cool the milk/cream and agar mix down to 40°C.

Add the lemon maple mixture and sprinkle in the starter culture (if using) and whisk together well.

Pour into warm (40°C) sterilised jars, cap and incubate, undisturbed for 4-6 hours.

Remove and refrigerate.

## Dairy-based yogurt
### Makes 1 litre

**1 litre full fat dairy milk**
**1 tsp sugar**
**2-3 tablespoons natural acidophilus yoghurt**

Pour the milk into a pot and gently heat, stirring regularly until it reaches 85°C.

Remove from the heat and stir in the sugar.

Continue stirring to prevent a skin forming until the liquid has cooled to 45°C. You can do this quickly by placing the pot into a bowl of ice.

Place the yoghurt in a bowl and whisk the milk mixture in a little at a time so it is incorporated evenly.

Pour into warm (40°C) sterilised jars, cap and incubate, undisturbed for 4-6 hours.

Remove and refrigerate.

# Pesto

I love pesto for its versatility. You can literally use any greens to make pesto from the traditional basil to silverbeet, rocket, coriander, nasturtium greens, dandelion greens, kale or a mix of all of these. Enjoy pesto as a dip, spread on bread, crackers or wraps, tossed through veggies, served with pies, quiches, tarts – the possibilities are endless!

*Vegan | Gluten free*
*Makes 1 cup*

**1 clove garlic, peeled**
**1/4 cup pine, macadamia or cashew nuts**
**2 cups leafy greens, herbs or edible weeds, chopped**
**1/4 cup hemp parmesan or Parmesan cheese, finely grated**
**zest and juice of 1 lemon**
**1/2 cup extra-virgin olive oil**
**1/2 tsp salt**
**a few grinds of pepper**

Place the garlic, nuts, greens, parmesan, lemon, olive oil, salt and pepper in a food processor. Whizz until finely chopped, scraping down the sides to ensure even consistency. I like quite chunky pesto but you can go for whatever consistency you prefer.

Alternatively, use a mortar and pestle to smash the garlic clove and salt together. Now add the macadamias and smash these up a little. Add the rest of the ingredients and smash up until mixed well together.

Keep in the fridge with the surface covered with olive oil to prevent browning.

# Balsamic Reduction

This recipe is one of my pantry staples and I absolutely love to use it on leafy green salads in the winter time. It coats the greens perfectly without destroying them with acidity which can happen with straight balsamic and it also compliments kale, silverbeet and abundant edible winter weeds which are a bit more robust. Once cold, simply drizzle over your salad with an equal amount of olive oil and a little Himalayan salt, simple and absolutely delicious.

*Vegan | Gluten free*
*Makes 600ml*

**1 litre balsamic vinegar**
**1/2 cup unrefined cane sugar**
**1 stalk rosemary**
**1/2 red onion, diced or 1 clove garlic, sliced (optional)**

Place the balsamic vinegar, sugar, rosemary and onion in a pot. Stir while bringing to the boil then turn down to a simmer and cook for about 30 minutes until reduced by half. Stir every now and then.

Remove from the heat, it will thicken more while it cools. When cold, decant into a jar or bottle, through a sieve to remove the red onion or garlic.

# Mayonnaise

Making your own mayo means there are no added nasties, and it tastes better too. I've added an option for using aquafaba instead of egg yolks in the recipe. Aquafaba is the liquid that beans are cooked in. The most commonly used aquafaba is chickpea liquid, however, any bean liquid can be used this way. Cannellini and butterbeans have nice thick aquafaba which is perfect for this mayonnaise. I use a mini food processor to make mayonnaise, or a stick blender is also a good option. If you're making it by hand, use a big flattish bowl and put a damp cloth underneath so it doesn't skate around.

## Vegan | Gluten free
## Makes 2 cups (500ml)

2 egg yolks
2 tablespoons stoneground or Dijon mustard
1 clove garlic, crushed if whisking
1 tsp unrefined cane sugar
250ml rice bran or preferred neutral oil
100ml extra-virgin olive oil or additional rice bran or preferred neutral oil
zest of 1 lemon (optional)
2 tablespoons lemon juice or vinegar
1/2 tsp Himalayan salt
a few grinds of black pepper

## Vegan option
Replace egg yolks with:
120ml aquafaba
1/2 tsp cream of tartar

Place the egg yolks (or aquafaba), mustard, garlic and sugar in a food processor or bowl. Whisk or whizz together until pale and thickening. Slowly add the oil, a quarter cup at a time, ensuring that it is emulsified before adding more. (When all the oil has been added it should be very thick.)

Add the lemon zest (if using) and juice along with the vinegar, salt and pepper. Whizz together thoroughly then transfer to a jar and keep refrigerated. Homemade mayo keeps in the fridge well for a couple of weeks, as long as you use a clean spoon every time you use it.

# Jam Jar Dressings

A salad is always tastier if it has a good dressing. Having dressings at the ready makes life easier, especially in the summer when you just want to get back outside and enjoy the sun. These five dressings are really versatile and each makes enough for four salads. You can use them to dress just about any combo of fresh and cooked salads. Each comes with alternative options to make them vegan and they are all gluten free. I suggest using a 500–600ml jar to make the dressings in so there is enough head room for shaking. Make sure you dress salads just before eating them, as anything leafy will collapse once dressing is added. The dressings last in the fridge for at least a month.

## Vegan | Gluten free
## Each dressing recipe makes 400ml jar

To make the dressings, measure all the ingredients into the jar. Secure the lid and shake vigorously for 1 minute. Keep in the fridge and bring out 1 hour before using.

## Honey Mustard Dressing

2 tablespoons runny honey or alternative liquid sweetener
2 tablespoons stoneground mustard
zest and juice of 2 lemons
2 tablespoons apple cider vinegar
1 clove garlic, crushed
1 heaped tsp salt
1/4 tsp cracked black pepper
200ml extra-virgin olive oil

The trick with this one is to warm the jar first to melt the honey before adding the other ingredients. I prefer stoneground mustard in this dressing but any mustard can be used.

## Yoghurt Dressing

1/2 cup thick plain yoghurt, plant-based or dairy
2 cloves garlic, crushed
2 tsp unrefined sugar
1/2 cup lemon juice, plus the zest of the lemons
1/2 cup extra-virgin olive oil
1 tsp salt
1/4 tsp cracked black pepper

A great alternative to mayonnaise and a lot healthier, this dressing turns a simple green salad into a taste sensation.

## Orange Maple Chia Dressing

1/2 cup orange juice
juice of 1 lemon
2 tablespoons chia seeds
2 tablespoons maple syrup
2 tablespoons pomegranate molasses or tamarind paste
2 tablespoons apple cider vinegar
2 tablespoons hemp seed oil
1 tablespoon Dijon or yellow mustard
1 tablespoon fresh turmeric, finely grated
1 tablespoon finely grated fresh ginger
1 clove garlic, crushed
1/4 cup extra-virgin olive oil or almond oil
1 tsp salt
1/4 tsp cracked pepper

As well as thickening up this dressing, the chia seeds are little nutrient-packed power houses which makes this dressing not only delicious but super healthy too.

## Lime Miso Dressing

juice of 6 limes
1 clove garlic, crushed
1 tablespoon coconut nectar
1 tablespoon miso paste
1 tablespoon finely grated ginger
1 tablespoon rice or coconut vinegar
2 tablespoons light soy sauce, tamari or coconut aminos
2 tablespoons sweet or fermented chilli sauce or 1 fresh chilli, diced (optional)
2 tablespoons rice bran oil
1/4 cup toasted sesame oil
2 tablespoons chopped fresh coriander

An Asian-style dressing with its sweet, sour, hot and salty elements is perfect to use with any fresh Asian-style salad or slaw, as well as a marinade and dipping sauce for rice rolls.

## Passionfruit Dressing

2 passionfruit, pulp scooped out
1 tsp runny honey
1 heaped tsp stoneground mustard
zest and juice of 1 lime or lemon
2 tablespoons apple cider vinegar
200ml extra-virgin olive oil
1 tablespoon virgin sesame oil
1 tsp salt
a few grinds of pepper

Not only pretty with the passionfruit seeds, this tangy dressing is perfect with a simple summer salad.

# Veggie Stock

*Making your own veggie stock is super easy and well worth it. You basically save all your onion, carrot, celery, mushroom, tomato, capsicum, leek, corn cobs and beetroot scraps in a container or sealed bag in the freezer, and when it is full add to a pot with water and simmer for one hour. I like to add seaweed to mine as it is a great source of omega-3, iron, calcium, iodine, and vitamins it also has a thickening quality that mimics gelatine. You can also add garlic, ginger and turmeric for anti-inflammatory and antioxidant support as well as dried mushrooms for their depth of flavour and medicinal qualities. It's up to you whether you go for the roasting option, which will make the final stock darker and richer.*

### Vegan | Gluten free
### Makes 2.5 litres

2 whole onions, skin on and roughly chopped
1 whole leek, roughly chopped
1 whole bulb garlic, halved width ways
2 sticks of celery (plus the end and scrappy tops), roughly chopped
2 whole carrots, roughly chopped
1-2 beetroot, roughly chopped (optional)
2-3 sweetcorn cobs (optional)
2-3 tablespoons extra-virgin olive oil
400g tomatoes, halved, or tin tomatoes/passata
8cm piece fresh ginger, sliced
8cm piece fresh turmeric, sliced or 2 tablespoon turmeric powder
1/2 tsp black peppercorns
1 stick lemongrass, bruised
1 large stick fresh rosemary
4 bay leaves
8 (35g) dried or fresh mushrooms, shiitake, oyster, porcini or foraged
10g medicinal mushrooms, reishi, turkey tail, chaga or cordyceps (optional)
1-5 pieces dried seaweed, kombu, wakame or kelp
4 litres water

Preheat the oven to 200°C (You can also omit the roasting stage and just add ingredients to the pot).

Put the roughly chopped vegetables into a roasting tray, drizzle with the olive oil and roast for 10 minutes.

Place the remaining ingredients in a large pot.

Remove the vegetables from the oven and add to the pot along with the water.

Bring to the boil uncovered, then turn down to a simmer and cook for 1 to 1 1/2 hours. Remove from the heat, strain and pour into warm sterilised jars and cap.

Store in the pantry like this, once opened store in the fridge.

TOFU SCRAMBLE WITH HASH BROWNS
AND SMOKY COCONUT CHIPS

PANCAKES

HOTCAKES AND WAFFLES SWEET AND SAVOURY

BRIOCHE PINWHEELS

MUFFINS

SWEET AND SAVOURY SPOON SCONES

GRANOLA

RAINBOW SMOOTHIES

# Breakfast / Brunch

# Tofu Scramble with Hash Browns & Smoky Coconut Chips

*This tofu scramble is quick, easy, soft and scrumptious! I love a good brunch and this combo really hits the spot. With crispy quick hash browns and smoky coconut chips, it's the perfect plant-based brunch or lunch with a little relish or hot sauce. Black salt really does make a tasty difference to this dish; it also has antioxidant properties along with important minerals iron, potassium, sulphur and has surprising low sodium levels.*

Vegan | Gluten free
Serves 4

## Tofu Scramble

300g block tofu, soft or firm
1/4 cup aquafaba
1/2 tsp ground turmeric
1/4 tsp black pepper
1/2 tsp salt or black salt (for a more 'eggy' flavour)
1/3 cup finely chopped onion weed, chives or parsley
2 tablespoons extra-virgin olive oil
1 onion, diced

## Hash Browns (Makes 15)

2 tablespoons ground flaxseed mixed in 1/3 cup water or 2 eggs
4 medium potatoes, scrubbed clean and grated
1/3 cup cornflour
1 tablespoon roughly chopped chives, onion flowers or sage
1/2 tsp salt
a few grinds of pepper
1/4 cup rice bran oil

## Smoky Coconut Chips

2 tablespoons light soy sauce, tamari or coconut aminos
2 tsp liquid smoke
1 tablespoon maple syrup
1 tablespoon smoked paprika
1/2 tsp Himalayan or flaked salt
4 cups coconut chips

To make the Tofu Scramble, place the tofu, aquafaba, turmeric, pepper, salt and herbs in a flat bowl and mash together well. Heat a cast-iron pan to medium-high heat and add the olive oil and onion. Slow sauté until soft but not coloured, about 8 minutes. Add the tofu mix and cook gently, stirring constantly for 2 minutes and serve on top of hash browns (recipe below) and top with freshly diced tomato or green pea micro-greens and smoky coconut chips (recipe below).

To make the Hash Browns, start with making the flax egg (if using) by mixing the ground flaxseeds with the water and leaving to absorb for 5 minutes (stir once during this time). Place the flax egg or eggs, potato, cornflour, herbs, salt and pepper in a bowl and stir to combine. Heat 2 tablespoons of oil for each round of hash browns in a cast-iron pan or hot plate on a barbeque. Scoop 1 tablespoon of the mix at a time into the pan or the hotplate on a medium-high heat. Push it flat with the back of the spoon and cook the first side until golden brown before flipping over, making sure your pan is hot, but not so hot that it will burn your hash. When both sides are golden, take it out of the pan and place it on a cooling rack to keep crisp. Repeat with the rest of the mixture.

To make the Coconut Chips, line an oven tray with baking paper and preheat the oven to 150°C. Place the soy sauce, liquid smoke, maple syrup, smoked paprika and salt into a mixing bowl and stir to combine. Then add the coconut chips and gently mix well to coat evenly and spread out on the prepared tray in one layer. Bake for 10 minutes, stirring once. These burn easily, so turn your timer on! When cold, store in a jar to keep crisp.

# Pancakes

*Whether you are a sweet or savoury breakfast kind of person, this versatile recipe will tick all the boxes. And you don't just need to limit yourself to breakfast either, I love to roll savoury fillings in pancakes, as you would for cannelloni, then bake with a sauce or a sprinkle of cheese for a lunch or dinner. I recommend using a cast-iron pan for pancakes as the heat is more evenly dispersed which cooks the pancakes evenly. It is essential to look after your cast-iron pans, here are a couple of tips. Never leave it sitting in a sink of water, always clean immediately after use, dry and rub with oil before storing, this will keep your pan non-stick and make it last a lifetime.*

## Vegan | Gluten free
## Serves 4

2 cups wholemeal flour (spelt if you can find it)
a pinch of salt
1 egg
2 cups milk, plant-based or dairy
3/4 cup water
4 tablespoons butter, dairy or plant-based, or 4 tablespoons coconut oil, virgin or refined

## Gluten-free option

Replace wholemeal flour with:
1 1/2 cup sorghum or buckwheat flour or a mixture of both
1/3 cup cornflour or potato flour

## Vegan option

Replace egg with:
2 tablespoons ground flaxseeds mixed with 1/4 cup water (leave to absorb for 10 minutes)

Measure the flours and salt into a large bowl. Make a well in the centre and add the egg or flax egg, milk and water. Whisk together, gradually incorporating from the centre out, until smooth. Add 2 tablespoons of butter and whisk through, leave the batter to sit for 30 minutes.

Heat a cast-iron pan and add a little butter, half a teaspoon at a time. When sizzling, add a ladle of the mixture to the pan and tip the pan around so the surface is completely covered with batter. Loosen at the edges with a spatula and flip the pancake over when it's golden on the first side, then cook the other side for another 30 seconds.

Stack the pancakes on a plate. Repeat until all the mix has been used.

# Hotcakes and Waffles
## Sweet and Savoury

*Light and fluffy, this versatile recipe can be made both sweet and savoury, plain or with blueberries or cheese added to the mix to satisfy everyone's tastes. A firm family favourite, it is a nice big recipe for when you have a full house, but feel free to halve it. However, I always find that no matter how many I make, they disappear pretty fast. The batter can be kept in the fridge for a couple of days.*

## Vegan | Gluten free
### Makes 50 x 8 cm hotcakes or 20 large hotcakes or waffles

4 cups plain flour, sifted
1/4 cup cornflour
4 heaped tsp baking powder
2 3/4 cup milk, plant-based or dairy
2 tsp vanilla extract (sweet version only)
1/4 cup maple syrup (sweet version only)
4 egg yolks
4 egg whites
60g melted butter, plant-based or dairy (reserve 2 tablespoons for cooking) or 1/4 cup coconut oil (reserve 2 tablespoons for cooking)
250g blueberries (optional)
250g cheese, plant-based or dairy, grated (optional)

### Gluten-free option
Replace flour and cornflour with:
4 cups gluten-free flour mix

### Vegan option
Replace egg yolks with:
2 bananas, mashed or 1/4 cup aquafaba

Replace egg whites with:
 or 1 cup aquafaba (brine) with 1 tsp cream of tartar

Replace butter with:
1/4 cup coconut oil (reserve 2 tablespoons for cooking)

Measure the flour, cornflour (or gluten-free flour mix) and baking powder into a large mixing bowl. Measure the milk, vanilla extract and maple syrup (only for the sweet version) into a jug, then add the egg yolks (or banana or aquafaba) and whisk together well.

In a clean bowl, beat the egg whites (or aquafaba and cream of tartar) until soft peaks form, about 5 minutes. Make a well in the centre of the mixing bowl and pour the contents of the jug and the melted butter (or alternatives) into the mixing bowl. Whisk together until smooth then fold in the beaten egg whites or aquafaba and either blueberries or grated cheese (if using).

To make as hotcakes, heat a hotplate or frying pan to a medium-high heat and add a little melted butter before each batch. When the surface of the hotcakes are bubbling flip each one over and cook for 45 seconds to 1 minute. Flip again to ensure they are cooked through. Lightly press the top, it should bounce back. Remove from the heat to a cooling rack and repeat until all the batter has been used.

To make as waffles, turn on the waffle iron and brush the top and bottom with melted butter. Ladle in the batter, draping it in the shape of the iron to ensure even cooking and close the lid. When the waffles are golden brown remove and repeat until all the batter has been used.

# Brioche Pinwheels

A delicious, enriched bread dough, brioche is the ultimate Christmas breakfast treat! They can be made the night before and left to slowly prove (rise) in the fridge overnight. Be sure to bring them out to come to room temperature for at least an hour before baking. This recipe has a cornflour-based custard as it has a firmer texture which holds its shape inside the pinwheel. If kneading by hand, this dough is sticky and soft, refrain from adding too much flour to stop it sticking. Just keep kneading and working it and use a dough scraper or spatula to help move it to the bowl.

## Vegan | Gluten free
## Makes 8 pinwheels

1/2 tsp active yeast granules
2 tablespoons sugar
1/2 cup milk, plant-based or dairy, gently warmed
150g butter, plant-based or dairy or 1/2 cup coconut oil, virgin or refined, melted
2 eggs, whisked or 1 banana, mashed
2 1/2 cup plain or high-grade flour
Small pinch of salt
1 egg or 2 tablespoons soy milk, to glaze

### Gluten-free option

2 cup warm milk, plant-based or dairy
1/2 cup psyllium husk
1/2 cup ground flaxseed
1 cup brown rice flour, sorghum or buckwheat flour
1/2 cup sorghum, brown rice flour or buckwheat
1/2 cup tapioca or potato flour
2 tsp baking powder
small pinch salt

### Custard

2 tablespoons cornflour
1 tablespoon maple syrup
1 tsp vanilla paste
1/2 tsp ground cinnamon
2 cups milk, dairy or almond
1/4 cup raisins
1/4 cup dried cranberries

## Filling

1 apple, peeled and cored, then diced
zest and juice of 1 lemon
1 apricot, peach or plum, stone removed and diced
1 tablespoon sugar, raw, coconut or brown
1 tsp ground cinnamon
1/4 cup chopped almonds
1 egg or 2 tablespoons soy milk

Measure the yeast, sugar and milk into a mixing bowl and rapidly mix with your hand. Add the butter and eggs and mix in. Add the flour and salt, using hook attachment of your electric mixer, mix for 5 minutes. Alternatively, use a butter knife to bring the elements of the dough together, then use the heel of your hands to knead it until it is smooth and soft. Tip the dough into the pan in which you melted the butter and turn it several times to coat. Return the dough to the mixing bowl and cover with a damp tea towel. Set aside to prove until it has doubled in size, about 2 hours depending on the ambient temperature. Line a large tray with baking paper.

To make the custard, measure the cornflour, maple syrup, vanilla paste and ground cinnamon into a pot. Add 1/4 cup of the milk to the pan and stir well. Add the remaining milk and put onto a medium heat. Stir constantly until thick. Remove from the heat and measure in the raisins and cranberries. Mix well and pour into a dish, cover with a disk of baking paper or cling film to prevent a skin forming while it cools. Refrigerate until needed.

To make the filling, place apple, lemon zest and juice, apricot (or peach or plum) in a pan. Cover and cook on a low heat for 4 minutes until soft. Remove from the heat and set aside. Combine the sugar, ground cinnamon and almonds in a small bowl.

When the dough has doubled in size, tip it out onto a floured bench and push the dough out into a rectangle shape, about 35 x 20cm.

Spread the custard evenly over two-thirds of the dough, leaving one long edge clear. Spread the apple over the custard and sprinkle over 2 tsp of the sugar and cinnamon mix.

Whisk the egg (or soy milk) and brush onto the clear edge. Start rolling the dough from the opposite edge to this, lifting slightly and tucking the edge under as you roll. It is soft and a little tricky to do, try not to squeeze the filling out. Finish on the egg-washed edge and roll over so the seam is underneath.

Use a sharp knife to cut the roll in half, hold the roll while you are doing this. Saw a little to cut the top then push the knife through in one movement right to the bench. Cut each half in half again, to make four pieces, then once more to make eight.

Carefully transfer the pinwheels to a baking tray. Place cut-side down, arranging evenly on the tray, either one in the middle and seven around the edges or line them up with 1cm between each to give them enough space to prove. Cover with a damp tea towel and leave to prove again until doubled in size, 1–2 hours.

Preheat the oven to 180°C. Brush the pinwheels with the leftover egg mix then top with the remaining sugar and cinnamon mix. Bake for 20–30 minutes until golden. Another option for a filling is cherry and chocolate. Spread some jam over the dough first then add an equal measure of chocolate to cherries (pitted) and combine before distributing over the dough.

# Muffins

*This recipe is very versatile, you can make it sweet or savoury, or use your choice of fruit or vegetable to flavour the muffins. Some suggestions to use are mashed bananas, berries, cut stone fruit, grated apple, pear, carrot or zucchini. If using zucchini, squeeze some of the excess water out before adding. You can also substitute one cup of an alternative flour into the recipe. I like using oat flour, you can make your own by whizzing up oats in the food processor.*

## Vegan | Gluten free
## Makes 12 regular or 24 minis

1 cup prepared fruit or vegetable
2 cups wholemeal flour, sifted
2 heaped tsp baking powder, sifted
1 egg
60g butter
200–220ml milk, plant-based or dairy
1 tablespoon apple cider vinegar
1/4 cup virgin coconut oil or butter, plant-based or dairy, melted

## Sweet version

1/4 cup coconut sugar
1 tsp vanilla extract
150g dark chocolate, cut up into chunks (optional)

## Savoury version

1/2 cup grated cheese
1 tablespoon oregano, dried

## Gluten-free version

Replace flour and eggs with:
1/3 cup brown rice flour
1/3 cup sorghum or buckwheat flour
1/3 cup almond flour
1/3 cup cornflour, tapioca or potato flour
1 tablespoon chia seeds mixed with 1/4 cup water

Preheat the oven to 190°C. Prepare the chia mix (if using) and melt the coconut oil or butter. Brush the muffin tins with the melted oil.

Add the prepared fruit or vegetables to the dry ingredients and stir through, followed by the chia seed mix or the egg and the wet ingredients. Stir until just combined, then spoon into the prepared muffin tins and top with a slice of the fruit used (optional) and a sprinkle of sugar (for the sweet version).

Bake for 10–15 minutes until a skewer inserted comes out clean. Cool for 4 minutes before removing from the tins onto a cooling rack.

# Sweet and Savoury Spoon Scones

*Another versatile everyday recipe, I invented these spoon scones for my kids' cooking classes. Using a spoon to scoop the mix out of the bowl and another to slide it on to the tray makes these scones less messy. No wiping up floury benches and no need for a rolling pin or shaping. I love having a scone base to embellish any way you please. Whether you are a sweet or savoury lover these will hit the spot for a quick morning tea or snack which the kids can help you make in a jiffy. Pictured are the plain sweet versions with homemade apricot jam and whipped coconut cream, perfect with a cup of tea.*

## Vegan | Gluten free
### Makes 10 –12 scones

2 cups wholemeal spelt or plain flour
2 heaped tsp baking powder
50g butter, plant-based or dairy
1 cup milk: dairy, oat or rice

## Gluten-free option

Replace wholemeal spelt or plain flour with:
1/2 cup brown rice flour
1/2 cup sorghum or buckwheat
1/3 cup tapioca or potato flour
2 heaped tsp baking powder
1/3 cup psyllium husk mixed with 1/2 cup warm milk
1/2 cup extra milk for mixing

## Savoury

2 tsp poppy seeds or 2 tsp oregano, dried or fresh, roughly chopped
1/2 cup cheese, plant-based or dairy, grated, plus
1/4 cup more for the tops
1/2 tsp salt
1/4 tsp cracked black pepper

## Sweet

1/2 cup dates, chopped
3 tablespoons coconut sugar

Preheat the oven to 190°C. Line an oven tray.

Sift the flour(s) and baking powder into a bowl. Add the butter and rub into the flour using your fingertips until breadcrumb consistency. Then add sweet or savoury flavourings (if using) and stir in. Add the milk or psyllium mixture and stir until it forms one mass, mixing in the second measure of milk as you stir.

Using two spoons, scoop the mixture onto the tray using one spoon to pick up the mixture and the other spoon to help push it onto the tray. Leave a 2cm gap between each and repeat until all the mixture has been used. Brush the top of each scone with milk and bake for 15 minutes until golden brown.

# Granola

*Fruity, nutty, crunchy and packed with goodness this granola is perfect layered with yoghurt and fresh fruit or a generous pour of your favourite milk. It hits the spot at breakfast, brunch or even the three o'clock hunger pangs. This granola uses puffed gluten-free grains instead of oats and it's totally up to you to choose your favourite fruit and nuts to add for ultimate satisfaction.*

## Vegan | Gluten free
## Makes 6 cups

1/2 cup coconut or preferred oil
1/2 cup maple or date syrup
1 tablespoon ground cinnamon
1 tablespoon vanilla extract
2 cups quinoa, amaranth, buckwheat or millet puffs (or a combined mixture of all four)
2 cups nuts and seeds (e.g. coconut chips, almonds, hazelnuts, cashew pieces, walnuts, sunflower seeds, pumpkin seeds, hemp seeds), sliced or roughly chopped
1 1/2 cup dried fruit (e.g. dates, apricots, figs, raisins or cranberries), roughly chop larger pieces
1/3 cup cacao nibs

Preheat the oven to 150°C. Measure the coconut oil and syrup into a pot and heat on a low temperature until the coconut oil has melted (omit this step if using a liquid oil, whisk the oil and syrup together). Add the cinnamon and vanilla, stir through.

Measure the puffs and nuts/seeds into a large tray, then pour the oil and syrup mixture into the tray and stir together to coat. Bake for 30 minutes, until dry to the touch, stir every 10 minutes to make sure it all toasts evenly.

Remove the tray from the oven, add the dried fruit and cacao nibs and stir through, leave to cool.

Store in a jar or cereal tin.

# Rainbow Smoothies

Smoothies are a great way to add a whole lot of goodness to our diet. They can also be made into heathy puddings by simply adding chia seeds and putting them in the fridge to thicken. Another idea is to layer them with some fresh fruit to give a bit of texture and add something crunchy to the top such as cereal flakes, granola, coconut or banana chips. Any excess smoothies can be frozen into homemade ice blocks. My girls prefer to enjoy smoothies this way. There are many superfood powders such as maca available on the market today which are packed full of vitamins and minerals. A great way to benefit from these is to add them to smoothies. Smoothies will last up to one week in a sealed jar in the fridge, shake well before using.

## Vegan | Gluten free

### Each colour makes I litre

Combine ingredients in a blender, or in a jug with stick blender, and process until smooth.

### Blue

1 cup blueberries
1 banana
2 cups chopped white nectarine, lychee or extra banana
2 cups apple juice or coconut water
1 cup plain yoghurt, plant-based or dairy
1 tablespoon maple syrup

### White

3 bananas
1 cup plain yoghurt, plant-based or dairy
2 tsp maca powder (optional)
1 tablespoon honey or maple syrup
1/2 tsp ground cinnamon
2 cups milk, plant-based or dairy

### Pink

2 cups strawberries, hulled
2 cups chopped watermelon
1 cup raspberries
2 cups coconut water
1 tablespoon vanilla paste
2–3 tablespoons maple syrup (optional, if berries are frozen or not fully ripe)

### Yellow

150ml coconut milk
2 cups chopped mango flesh or purée
4 passionfruit, pulp or 1/2 cup papaya flesh
2 tsp fresh turmeric, grated
2 cups almond milk
zest and juice of 2 limes

### Orange

500ml grapefruit juice (4–6 grapefruit)
2 bananas, peeled
1 cup yoghurt, plant-based or dairy
2 tablespoons finely grated fresh turmeric
2 tablespoons finely grated fresh ginger
1/2 cup mango (optional)
1–2 tablespoons manuka honey or alternative sweetener
1/2 tsp black pepper
2 sprigs mint

### Green

2 avocados, skin and stone removed, chopped
1 kiwifruit, skin removed, chopped
2 1/2 cups apple juice or coconut water
1 tablespoon spirulina powder or hemp protein powder
1–2 leaves silverbeet or kale, stem removed, roughly chopped
1–2 tablespoons maple syrup (optional)

*Smoothie Bowl*

## Brown

8 medjool dates, stones removed
2 cups milk, plant-based or dairy
1 cup raw cashew nuts, softened
3 tablespoons cacao powder
2 tablespoons maple syrup
1 cup ice cubes

## Purple

2 cups blackberries
1 cup cherries, pitted or blackcurrants
1 tablespoon organic blackstrap molasses
3 tablespoons maple, coconut or agave syrup
2 cups apple juice

## Options

• If you want to make smoothie bowls, freeze the fruit first, blend, spoon into a bowl then top with fresh fruit and crunchy elements for texture.

• To quickly chill smoothies, add one cup of ice to the recipe before blending.

• To make into chia puddings, use 1 cup smoothie to 3 tablespoons chia seeds. Chill for 4 hours or overnight in the fridge.

WINTER SLAW WITH TAMARI PUMPKIN AND SUNFLOWER SEEDS
SUMMER SLAW
CAULIFLOWER, CASHEW AND CHICKPEA SLAW
CURRIED KUMARA AND ROASTED CAULIFLOWER SALAD
GREEN BEANS WITH CRISPY SAGE AND HAZELNUTS
PASTA SALAD
SUPER SALAD
HONEY ROAST CARROT AND PARSNIP SALAD
FENNEL AND RADICCHIO SALAD
BEETROOT AND BLUE CHEESE SALAD
HALLOUMI, COUSCOUS AND ORANGE SALAD
CHUNKY VEGETABLE SOUP
THAI PUMPKIN AND CASHEW SOUP
MUSHROOM SOUP WITH SAUTÉED GARLIC MUSHROOMS
GAZPACHO WITH QUINOA-FILLED AVOCADOS
CREAM OF SWEETCORN SOUP
BORSCHT

# Salads and Soups

# Winter Slaw with Tamari Pumpkin and Sunflower Seeds

*I love winter vegetables in salads, they are crunchy, juicy and delicious! This salad is the perfect balance to the winter comfort food we all crave at that time of year – it refreshes the palate with a good dose of raw veg. I very rarely peel vegetables as the nutrients are usually found in or just under the skin. I give them a quick scrub to clean off any soil. You can really have a bit of free will with this salad regarding what veggies you put in, depending on tastes and availability. Utilising the wild weeds in the garden is empowering and free, so I have added some options for those who would like to add these to the salad for extra nutrition and flavour.*

*I always have a jar of the Tamari Pumpkin and Sunflower Seeds in the pantry. They add a lovely crunchy saltiness to leafy and grainy salads and make a great snack in between meals too.*

## Vegan | Gluten free
## Serves 4–6

1/4 cabbage, red or white, finely sliced
1 cup finely sliced silverbeet or kale (about 4–5 leaves and stems)
4–5 florets cauliflower or broccoli, finely sliced
1–2 sticks celery, finely sliced
2 radishes, finely sliced
1 carrot, grated
1 parsnip or beetroot, grated
1 apple or yacon, grated
juice of 1 lime
2 stems fresh parsley, finely chopped
1/2 cup onion weed, dandelion, chicory, oxalis or plantain leaves, finely chopped (optional)
1/2 cup sprouts, alfalfa, mung bean, broccoli, lentil (optional)
2 gherkins, diced
1 tablespoon capers (optional)
3 tablespoons raisins or cranberries
1/2 tsp Himalayan pink salt
1/2 cup Mayonnaise (page 40)
1/2 cup Tamari Pumpkin and Sunflower Seeds or walnuts
a few grinds of black pepper

Place all the ingredients in a large salad bowl. Toss together well and serve.

## Tamari Pumpkin and Sunflower Seeds
## (Makes 4 1/2 cups)

2 cups pumpkin seeds
2 cups sunflower seeds
1/2 cup sesame seeds
3 tablespoons light soy sauce, tamari or coconut aminos

To make the Tamari Pumpkin and Sunflower Seeds, preheat the oven to 180°C and measure the seeds into a roasting dish. Cook for 15 minutes, turning a couple of times. When they are beginning to colour, add the soy sauce and stir in then pop the tray back in the oven for 1 minute. Take the tray out and cool the seeds completely before using or storing in a jar.

# Summer Slaw

Great with burgers, this juicy and creamy summer slaw is perfect for a barbeque. I love to enjoy raw sweetcorn straight off the cob when they are at their best and find no need to cook them first. However, if they are past their best you may need to give them a quick steam to revive them.

*Vegan | Gluten free*
*Serves 4-6*

1 cob sweetcorn, kernels only
1 bulb fennel or 2 sticks celery, finely sliced
10 fresh yellow, green or purple beans, finely sliced
1 yellow or orange capsicum, diced
1 spring onion, finely sliced
1 zucchini, sliced into matchsticks or spiralised
1/4 telegraph/Lebanese cucumber, sliced into matchsticks or spiralised
2 sprigs dill, roughly chopped
2 sprigs basil, roughly chopped
1/4 cup Mayonnaise (page 40)
1/2 tsp salt
a few grinds of pepper
1/4 cup Smoky Coconut Chips (optional, page 48)

Prepare the vegetables and herbs and place in a bowl. Add the mayonnaise and seasoning and toss together well. Top with the Smoky Coconut Chips.

# Cauliflower, Cashew and Chickpea Slaw

This salad is definitely a favourite. The addition of cashew nuts and chickpeas means it doesn't only taste great, it is protein- and fibre-packed as well as being high in iron, magnesium and vitamins.

*Vegan | Gluten free*
*Serves 4-6*

1/2 cauliflower, cut into rough chunks (4 cups)
1 cup raw cashew nuts
1 clove garlic, peeled
1/2 cup chickpeas, sprouted or cooked
1/4 red cabbage, finely sliced, then sliced in half again
2 sticks of celery, thinly sliced
1 orange or tangelo, peeled and sliced (optional)
1 avocado, diced (optional)
zest and juice of 1 lime
1/2 cup finely chopped fresh parsley and mint
1/2 tsp salt
a few grinds of black pepper
1/3 cup Mayonnaise (page 40)

Place the cauliflower, cashew nuts and garlic in a food processor and pulse together until it resembles couscous. Tip out into a salad bowl and add the chickpeas, red cabbage, celery, orange, avocado, lime, herbs, salt and pepper. Mix together then add the mayonnaise and stir through.

Cauliflower, Cashew and Chicpea Slaw

# Curried Kumara and Roasted Cauliflower Salad

This creamy, hearty salad has many layers of flavours and textures making it perfect to take for a potluck dinner, a barbeque or even as a meal in itself. I've roasted the kumara and cauliflower but you could also steam them, if preferred. The crispy lentils are totally delicious and you may like to make a little more as they are very moreish! At the end of winter and early spring, onion flowers are coming out and they truly are the first spring onions, plus their little white flowers make a beautiful edible garnish. Ruruhau is a mustardy, open, cabbage-type green which is native to New Zealand but any punchy mustardy green is perfect.

*Vegan | Gluten free*
*Serves 4*

1/2 cup brown or green lentils
2 cups water
2–3 red kumara, cut into bite-sized pieces
3 tablespoons coconut or rice bran oil
1 tablespoon cumin seeds
1/2 tsp salt
1/4 tsp black pepper
1/2 cauliflower, cut into floret
2 tablespoons coconut or rice bran oil
4 sticks celery, sliced
6 spring onions or onion weed, sliced
2 cups chopped greens (ruruhau, mustard greens, mizuna, young turnip or radish leaves)
1/2 cup raisins (optional)
1/2 cup cashew nuts (optional)
3 gherkins, sliced (optional)
350ml Mayonnaise (page 40)
2 tsp curry powder, mild or hot
1 clove garlic, crushed

Preheat the oven to 180 °C. Measure the lentils and water into a pot, then cover and cook for 20 minutes. Once cooked, strain and leave to drain.

Prepare the kumara and place in a roasting tray. Add the first measure of oil, cumin seeds, salt and pepper. Toss together and roast for 15 minutes, turning once during cooking. Increase the heat to 200°C and add the cauliflower, toss through and bake for a further 14 minutes. Leave to cool.

Heat the second measure of oil in a roasting pan along with the lentils and a pinch of salt. Bake for 15 minutes. Place the celery, spring onions and greens in a salad bowl, then add the raisins, cashew nuts and gherkins (if using), and the roasted vegetables. Mix the mayonnaise, curry powder and garlic together.

Serve the salad with the dressing and topped with the roasted, crispy lentils.

# Green Beans with Crispy Sage and Hazelnuts

*This tasty little side dish could be adapted for any variety of fresh beans or greens and is quick and easy to prepare. The hazelnuts and crispy sage are a match made in heaven, crispy and crunchy, earthy and satisfying. I don't often bother to remove the skins from hazelnuts and this is where a lot of the antioxidants are. Hazelnuts are also high in omega-3s as well as heart healthy phenolic compounds which reduce inflammation and cholesterol. This side dish would be perfect with gnocchi, pasta, a ragu, casserole or stew.*

## Vegan | Gluten free
## Serves 4

1/4 cup extra-virgin olive oil
1/2 cup hazelnuts
1 large shallot, peeled and finely sliced
500g beans, tails removed and sliced on the diagonal into bite-sized pieces
1 tablespoon butter, plant-based or dairy
20 fresh sage leaves
juice of 1 lemon
1/2 tsp flaky or Himalayan pink salt
a few grinds of black pepper

Gently heat the oil in a cast-iron frying pan and add the hazelnuts. Toast over a medium heat for 4 minutes. Add the shallot to the pan and fry for 6–8 minutes until it is beginning to caramelise and the hazelnuts are golden.

Meanwhile, put the beans onto steam with a pinch of salt for 3–4 minutes until bright green and just tender, remove from the heat and briefly pass under cold water to stop cooking (this ensures the bright green colour remains). Shake off excess water and place in a serving bowl.

Remove the hazelnuts and shallots from the pan with a slotted spoon and add to the green beans. Add butter and sage leaves to the pan and fry until crispy, turning with tongs to ensure even cooking.

Pour the crispy leaves, excess oil and melted butter over the greens, add a squeeze of lemon, season and serve.

# Pasta Salad

*This is the most simple pasta salad ever, but sometimes with family food simple is best. These fun tri-colour pasta shapes are coloured with vegetables and are easily found in supermarkets. Any pasta will do though – gluten-free, paleo or wholemeal. Even if you have a tiny patch of garden or only a pot you will be able to grow some calendula or borage. Once you have it, it pops up year after year in the craziest places. Nasturtiums and onion weed grow wild all over New Zealand and there are pictures to reference in this book so you can be sure of what you are gathering. You can also buy edible flowers in some stores and markets. Additional options could be feta cheese, any leftover grilled or roasted vegetables, pesto, sliced beans or snow peas, avocado chunks, olives or sprouted pulses.*

## Vegan | Gluten free
## Serves 4

1 tsp salt
300g dried pasta shapes of choice
2 tablespoons extra-virgin olive oil
400g can chickpeas, drained and rinsed
4–5 tomatoes, sliced into bite-sized pieces or 1 cup cherry tomatoes, halved
1/2 cup edible flowers and weeds or fresh herbs such as chives, basil, dill or parsley
1/4 cup extra-virgin olive oil
1 tsp flaked sea salt
1/4 tsp cracked black pepper

Put a large pan of water on to boil. Once the water has come to the boil, add the salt and pasta. Cook the pasta as per instructions until just cooked, then empty into a colander in the sink.

Transfer the cooked pasta to a bowl and drizzle with the olive oil. Add the chickpeas, tomatoes, edible flowers, weeds and herbs, olive oil, salt and pepper. Toss together well and top with a few extra petals.

# Super Salad

*This salad is my go to for events and pot-luck dinners. It is nutritious, filling and pleases all dietary requirements. Packed with nutrients, this salad is pretty much a meal in a bowl. Roasting the root vegetables creates a depth of flavour and texture. Edible flower options include nasturtium (flowers and leaves), borage, calendula, onion weed or pansy flowers. Sprouts are also a fantastic edible garnish, options include mung bean, lentil, alfalfa, broccoli, red clover, radish or kale sprouts. To prepare sprouts: soak dried pulses or seeds overnight in a covered container, drain the next morning through a sieve, then leave in the sieve and cover with a tea towel. Rinse the beans again that night, then again next morning until they sprout. They are now ready to use.*

## Vegan | Gluten free
## Serves 10

1 cup quinoa, rinsed
1 1/2 cup water
1 tsp salt
1 tablespoon extra-virgin olive oil
1 cup medium grain brown rice or wild rice, rinsed
1/3 cup raisins or cranberries (optional)
650ml water
1/2 tsp salt
2 tablespoons extra-virgin olive oil
2 tablespoons rice bran oil
1 tsp sesame oil
1 stick of rosemary, leaves removed and roughly chopped
1/4 of a pumpkin, remove seeds and skin or 1 kumara, diced
2 capsicums, core removed, deseeded and large dice
1/2 tsp cracked black pepper
1/2 tsp salt
1/2 of a cauliflower or broccoli
3 radishes, sliced
1 punnet cherry tomatoes
1 cup tamari pumpkin and sunflower seeds (page 66)
1 bunch spring onion or a handful of onion weed spring onions, sliced
1 cup finely chopped herbs, parsley, coriander, plantain or dandelion leaves, finely chopped
1/2 cup honey mustard or orange chia dressing (page 42)
1 cup sprouts, mung bean, lentil and/or pea
1/2 cup edible flowers

Measure the quinoa, first measure of water, salt and olive oil into a pot. Cover with a lid and bring to the boil then turn down to a simmer and cook for 15 minutes. Stir with a fork then turn off the heat and leave to steam for 5 minutes.

In another pot put the rice, raisins, second measure of water and salt, cover and bring to the boil, then turn down to simmer for 20-25 minutes (until you can't see the water any more). Stir with a fork, put the lid back on, remove from the heat and leave the rice to steam for 10 minutes.

Tip out into a large bowl to help cool quickly, mix with a fork to separate grains and add the second measure of olive oil.

Preheat the oven onto 200°C. Add the rice bran oil, sesame oil, rosemary, pumpkin, capsicum, salt and pepper to a roasting tray, toss together and roast for 20 minutes, turning once during this time. Add the cauliflower, stir through and return to the oven for 10 minutes. Remove from the oven and cool.

To assemble, add cooled grains, roasted vegetables, radishes, cherry tomatoes, seeds, spring onion, herbs, dressing and sprouts into a large bowl and toss together well and check the seasoning. Top with edible flowers and serve.

# Honey Roast Carrot and Parsnip Salad

*This salad is one I used to make for café counters and really makes the most of winter vegetables. Cooked carrots and parsnips don't need to be boring and roasting them together with these delicious flavours really make them sing. I adore roasted brassicas, like cauliflower and broccoli especially if they have a few charred bits! The juicy citrus is totally optional, you could also use tomato if you prefer.*

## Vegan | Gluten free
## Serves 4-6

4 carrots, topped and tailed and sliced lengthways
4 parsnips, topped and tailed and sliced lengthways
2 tablespoons extra-virgin olive oil
2 tsp toasted sesame oil
1/2 tsp salt
1/4 tsp cracked black pepper
1/2 cauliflower, cut into florets
1/2 broccoli, cut into florets
1 bunch asparagus or beans, sliced on the diagonal
1 cup cashew or macadamia nuts, roughly chopped
2 tablespoons honey or maple syrup
2 tangelos, oranges or grapefruit, skin removed and sliced into segments
2 tablespoons hemp hearts
10 nasturtium leaves, roughly chopped
5 curly kale leaves, roughly chopped
1/2 cup coriander leaves, roughly chopped
1/4 cup mint leaves, roughly chopped
1/2 cup Honey Mustard or Orange Maple Chia Dressing (page 42)

Preheat the oven to 180°C. Place the carrots and parsnips in a roasting dish, drizzle with olive oil and sesame oil then sprinkle with salt and pepper. Roast for 20 minutes.

Remove from the oven and add the cauliflower, broccoli, asparagus and nuts. Mix through and return to the oven for 10 minutes. Drizzle with the honey and return to the oven for a further 5 minutes.

Transfer to a salad bowl and add the tangelos, hemp hearts, nasturtium leaves, kale leaves, coriander, mint and dressing, toss through and serve.

# Fennel and Radicchio Salad

This fennel and radicchio salad is simple to make, crispy and refreshing. Radicchio is a beautiful red and white leafy veg, like a mix between an iceberg-type lettuce and a cabbage. It's related to chicory so it's slightly bitter which means it is great for digestion, as is the fennel. This salad is perfect to have as a side for those winter comfort meals.

I love pistachios and I love even more that you can buy them without the shell on now! They are such a tasty accompaniment to the fennel and radicchio and have an awesome array of health benefits including high levels of vitamin B6, vitamin E, polyphenols, antioxidants plus they are very high in protein for their size. I think I may love salads even more in the wintertime and this one is bangin'.

*Vegan | Gluten free*
*Serves 4*

Prepare the ingredients straight into a salad bowl. Toss together well and serve. I've garnished with some lovely little wild mustard flowers and fennel tops.

1 clove garlic, crushed
zest and juice of 1 lemon
zest and juice of 1 orange
3 tablespoons extra-virgin olive oil or hemp seed oil
1 tablespoon honey or coconut nectar
1–2 fennel bulbs, finely sliced
1 radicchio head, finely sliced
1/4 cup pistachios, shelled
4 onion weeds or 1 spring onion, finely sliced
a handful of coriander, roughly chopped
a handful of basil, dandelion tips, baby wild mustard
or nasturtium leaves, roughly chopped
1/2 tsp salt
1/4 tsp cracked black pepper

# Beetroot and Blue Cheese Salad

Beetroot is so juicy and delicious when raw and paired with creamy tangy blue cheese and earthy crunchy walnuts this super food salad is like a nutritious flavour bomb. Beetroot is a prebiotic and is high in fibre and great for your eye, blood and liver health. Walnuts are great for your heart are high in antioxidants, polyphenols and omega-3s. If you've never tried pomegranate molasses you are in for a treat, its intense tart flavour is eye poppingly delicious and is a match made in heaven with the beetroot. Depending on the time of year, there's options within the recipe for the addition of fresh fruit, this is totally optional but some crisp pear or pomegranate would take this salad to the next level.

*Vegan | Gluten free*
*Serves 4*

1/2 cup walnuts
2 tablespoons maple syrup
a pinch of salt
2 beetroot, scrubbed and grated
4 silverbeet, kale leaves or 6 beetroot tops, finely sliced
1/4 cup dried apricots or figs (dried or fresh), roughly chopped or cranberries (optional)
2 tablespoons Balsamic Reduction (page 39)
1 tablespoon pomegranate molasses
2 tablespoons extra-virgin olive oil
1/2 tsp salt
1/4 tsp cracked black pepper
1 pear, finely sliced or 2 fresh figs, quartered (optional)
150g blue cheese or aged cashew or plant-based cheese, generously sliced in wedges

Preheat the oven to 180°C. Measure the walnuts onto a lined oven tray and bake for 10 minutes. Add the maple syrup and a pinch of salt, stir through and return to the oven for 2 minutes. Remove and cool.

Place the beetroot and silverbeet in a bowl and add the dried fruit (if using), half the walnuts, balsamic reduction, pomegranate molasses, olive oil, salt and pepper to the bowl. Mix to combine.

Tip into a salad bowl or a platter and arrange the pear or figs (if using) and cheese on top then sprinkle over the remaining walnuts to finish. Serve with fresh bread.

# Halloumi, Couscous and Orange Salad

*Halloumi is so versatile and adds a great backbone to this salad. Alternatively, you could use a plant-based feta crumbled over to top or roughly chopped macadamia nuts. To make this salad gluten-free use quinoa in place of the couscous and to suit a paleo diet, use a whole cauliflower in place of the couscous.*

*Vegan | Gluten free*
*Serves 6*

1 cup wholemeal or regular couscous
1 clove garlic, crushed
2 tablespoons extra-virgin olive oil
1/2 tsp salt
1 1/2 cups boiling water
zest and juice of 1 lemon
4 cauliflower florets, whizzed in the micro food processor until it reaches a couscous-like consistency or sliced finely or 1 bulb Florence fennel, thinly sliced
200g chickpea sprouts (or cooked chickpeas)
1/2 cup hemp hearts (optional)
1–2 leaves kale or silverbeet, finely chopped
1 spring onion or 4 onion weed spring onions, sliced
1/2 cup finely chopped parsley, mint, chives, coriander, onion weed, dandelion or plantain leaves
2 oranges, zest and flesh, roughly diced
zest and juice of 1 lemon
1/2 cup olives, pitted and sliced (optional)
1 packet (200g) halloumi, sliced into 5mm slices then sliced in half again (to make rectangles) or dairy-free feta, crumbled
2 tablespoons extra-virgin olive oil
3 tablespoons extra-virgin olive oil or hemp seed oil
1/2 tsp salt
1/4 tsp cracked black pepper

Place the couscous, garlic, first measure of olive oil, salt, water and lemon in a heatproof bowl, cover and let stand for 10 minutes.

Meanwhile, place the cauliflower, chickpeas, hemp hearts (if using), kale, spring onion, herbs, oranges, lemon and olives in a bowl and toss together.

Place the halloumi in a bowl with the second measure of olive oil and heat a cast-iron pan, barbecue or hot plate until smoking hot. Place halloumi on the grill, pressing down to sear. Cook for 1 minute, check it has seared, then turn it over to grill the other side.

Add the halloumi to the bowl with the couscous. Drizzle with olive oil, season, toss together well and serve.

# Chunky Vegetable Soup

This soup is mighty wholesome and hearty; my version of a minestrone soup. It is a great recipe for using up all the little bits in your vegetable drawer. So don't worry if you don't have all the vegetables listed, just use what you have to hand. You'll need to prepare the sprouted lentils in advance. Soak dried lentils, green or brown, overnight covered in water. In the morning, drain through a sieve. Cover the sieve with a tea towel and rinse the beans again at night then again in the morning until little tails sprout out. They are now ready to use. If you haven't or don't want to sprout the lentils, just add them with the barley to the soaking water. If using the buckwheat groats for the gluten-free version, there's no need to soak these. You may need to cook the soup a little longer if you haven't soaked the barley.

## Vegan | Gluten free
## Serves 4-6

1/2 cup green or brown lentils, sprouted
1/2 cup pearled barley or buckwheat groats
1/4 cup extra-virgin olive oil
1 onion, diced
2 mushrooms, diced
1 carrot, diced
1 stick celery, sliced
1 parsnip, diced
1/2 leek, halved and sliced
2 cloves garlic, sliced
1 potato, diced
400g can chopped tomatoes or passata
1 tablespoon finely grated fresh ginger
1.6 litres liquid vegetable stock or water with 1 tsp vegetable bouillon stock powder
1/2 cup quinoa
1/4 cup wholemeal spaghetti, broken into pieces or any pasta shapes, gluten-free or other
1 tsp salt
a good few grinds of pepper
1 sprig rosemary, leaves finely chopped
1 tsp fresh or dried thyme leaves
5 sprigs fresh parsley, coriander, dandelion or plantain leaves, roughly chopped
2 tsp extra-virgin olive oil, per person
1 tablespoon parmesan, plant-based or dairy, per serve

Pre-prepare the lentil sprouts (if using). Soak the barley for up to 6 hours, if possible.

Put a large pot on a high heat and add the olive oil, onion, mushrooms, carrot, celery, parsnip, leek, garlic and potato and sauté for a couple of minutes.

Drain the soaked barley and add along with the tomatoes, ginger and stock. Gently simmer the soup with a lid on for 15 minutes.

Add the quinoa and pasta shapes and cook for a further 10 minutes, then season with salt and pepper and stir the fresh herbs and sprouts through.

Ladle into bowls and top each bowl with a drizzle of olive oil and sprinkle of parmesan before serving.

# Thai Pumpkin and Cashew Soup

*This soup is silky smooth with additions of jasmine rice for thickening and cashew for protein. Ginger and turmeric give a wonderful flavour, plus their anti-inflammatory, antioxidants, immune supporting properties are a bonus for winter chills. I use butternut pumpkin here, as it's a little easier to skin than most but any variety will work. Bruising the lemongrass helps to release the subtle flavour into your soup.*

## Vegan | Gluten free
## Serves 4-6

2 tablespoons coconut oil, virgin or refined
1 tsp sesame oil
1 leek or onion, roughly chopped
2 carrots, roughly chopped
1 stick celery, sliced
1 butternut pumpkin, peeled and chopped into pieces
2 cloves garlic, crushed
2 tablespoons mirin
400g coconut cream (reserve 3 tablespoons for serving)
1.6 litres liquid vegetable stock or water
1 thumb-sized piece fresh or frozen ginger, grated
1 thumb-sized piece fresh or frozen turmeric, grated, or 1 tablespoon dried
2 kaffir lime leaves or zest and juice of 1 lime (reserve lime juice to finish)
1/4 cup white jasmine rice
1/3 cup raw cashew nut pieces
2 tablespoons light soy sauce, tamari or coconut aminos
2 stalks lemongrass, bruised
5 sprigs fresh coriander, roughly chopped (add the roots if you have them along with the ginger and turmeric at the beginning of cooking)
1 tsp salt
1/4 tsp pepper
1 tsp chilli powder (optional)

Melt the coconut and sesame oil in a large pot on high heat, then add the leek, carrot, celery, pumpkin and garlic and sauté for 2 minutes.

Deglaze the pan with the mirin, stir through the mixture in the pan, then add the coconut cream, stock, ginger, turmeric, lime leaves or zest, rice, cashew nuts, soy sauce and lemongrass. Bring to the boil, then turn down to a simmer and cook for about 20 minutes, until the vegetables are soft and the rice is cooked.

Add the coriander and seasonings then cool before blending. Blend until smooth, then bring back to a simmer before serving.

# Mushroom Soup with Sautéed Garlic Mushrooms

*One for all the mushroom lovers! You can use any of your favourite mushrooms for this soup, bought, cultivated or foraged. You could substitute the aubergine for swede, turnip or parsnip, if preferred.*

## Vegan | Gluten free
### Serves 4-6

1 aubergine, diced
1 tsp salt
2 tablespoons extra-virgin olive oil
25g butter, plant-based or dairy
1 onion, diced
4 cups (350g) mushrooms
1 stick celery, sliced
1 small kumara, diced
4 cloves garlic, sliced
1/4 cup marsala (optional)
2 litres vegetable stock or water with 2 tsp vegetable bouillon stock powder
1 sprig rosemary, leaves finely chopped
2 tsp fresh or dried thyme leaves
1/3 cup roughly chopped hazelnuts or walnuts (optional)
1 tsp salt
1/2 tsp cracked black pepper
1/3 cup finely chopped parsley
100g blue cheese, diced (optional)

## Sautéed Garlic Mushrooms

2 tablespoons extra-virgin olive oil
25g butter, plant-based or dairy
4–6 button, Swiss brown or small portobello mushrooms, thickly sliced
4 cloves garlic, sliced
a pinch of salt
1/4 tsp pepper
1/4 cup finely chopped parsley

Place the aubergine in a colander, sprinkle with salt and leave to drain while you prepare the vegetables.

Heat the olive oil and butter in a large pot on a high heat. When the butter has melted, add the onion, mushrooms, celery, kumara, garlic and the aubergine which has been patted dry with a clean tea towel or similar. Sauté for 2 minutes then add the marsala, stir through, then add the vegetable stock, rosemary, thyme and nuts. Cover and bring to the boil, then turn down and simmer for 20 minutes.

Season and stir through the parsley and blue cheese (if using). Remove from the heat and cool before blending. Blend until very smooth and bring back to a simmer before serving.

Top with Sautéed Garlic Mushrooms and a sprinkle of parsley and a lick of Cashew Cream (page 24).

To make the Sautéed Garlic Mushrooms, heat the olive oil and butter in a pan on a high heat. When the butter has melted, add the mushrooms and sauté for 2 minutes. Turn the heat down to medium and add the garlic, sauté for a further 2 minutes. Add a dash of water, seasoning and the parsley and cook for a further minute. Remove from the heat. Serve on top of the mushroom soup.

# Gazpacho with Quinoa-filled Avocados

This recipe is fantastic for a hot summer's day and makes the most of lovely ripe tomatoes and summer's bounty. It is best served ice cold and ideal for making ahead of time, so it gets a chance to chill before serving. I find people are pleasantly surprised at how delicious this soup is once the initial shock of eating cold soup has subsided. As this dish is of Spanish origin, you could serve it with a Spanish Tortilla (page 124) for an alfresco lunch or even a picnic. It would travel well in a thermos to keep it cold.

## Vegan | Gluten free
### Serves 4-6

1 kg (8–10) tomatoes
2 slices bread, no crusts, torn into pieces
2 garlic cloves, peeled and roughly chopped
1 small red onion, roughly chopped
1/4 cup extra-virgin olive oil
1/4 cup red wine or balsamic vinegar
1 red capsicum, deseeded and chopped
1/4 cucumber, peeled and roughly chopped
1 tablespoon salt
1/2 tsp cracked black pepper

## Quinoa-filled Avocados

1/2 cup quinoa
250ml water
1/2 tsp salt
1/2 cup almonds
2 tsp cumin seeds
juice of 1/2 a lemon
1 tablespoon extra-virgin olive oil
1/2 tsp salt
a few grinds of black pepper
3 sprigs mint, leaves finely chopped
1/2 avocado per person (slice a flat edge on the bottom side of the avocado for stability)
2 tablespoons extra-virgin olive oil

Place all the soup ingredients in a bowl, stir together and leave to marinate for 1 hour, stirring a couple of times while marinating.

Meanwhile, place the quinoa, water and first measurement of salt in a pot and set it on the heat with a lid on and bring to the boil. Turn down to a simmer and cook for 8 minutes with the lid on until the water has absorbed. Stir once during cooking time. Remove from the heat and leave to steam for a couple of minutes, then remove the lid and stir to help cool.

Toast the almonds then the cumin seeds in a frying pan. Set aside to cool, then roughly chop. Place in a bowl with the cold quinoa and dress with the lemon, olive oil, salt, pepper and mint and stir together.

Tip the soup ingredients into a blender and blitz until smooth adding a quarter cup of cold water if needed. Push the blended mixture through a sieve into a large bowl. Discard all the seeds and skin left in the sieve. Check the seasoning then chill the smooth mixture in the fridge until ready to eat. Ladle the soup into bowls and top each bowl with one half of an avocado filled with the quinoa mix and a drizzle of extra-virgin olive oil.

# Cream of Sweetcorn Soup

*All the delicious flavour of sweetcorn without the bits, the taste of sunshine in a bowl! Along with the fresh flavour of lemongrass, and the immune supporting, antioxidants and anti-inflammatory properties of turmeric and ginger, it's the perfect soup for the change of seasons or to have at the ready for the cold season when you need a lift. I added some kelp gathered from the beach, dried and stored, to the stock in this batch for its high minerals, health benefits and it also gives soups a nice viscosity. Our chickens usually get the sweetcorn cobs but, as there is a lot of flavour still left in them, I decided to utilise them in the soup stock which you make as part of the recipe.*

## Vegan | Gluten free
## Serves 4-6

4 cobs sweetcorn
1 onion, peeled and roughly chopped
1 carrot, roughly chopped
1 yellow or orange capsicum, deseeded and roughly chopped
2 cloves garlic, sliced
2 stalks lemongrass, bruised
1 thumb-sized piece fresh turmeric, roughly chopped or 1 tablespoon ground turmeric
1 thumb-sized piece fresh ginger, roughly chopped
2 bay leaves
2 litres water
1 large potato or small kumara, scrubbed and roughly chopped
1 tsp salt
1/4 tsp pepper
1/2 tsp chilli powder (optional)
200ml cream, coconut or dairy
1 spring onion, thinly sliced

Break each corn cob in half and slice off the kernels with a sharp knife. Gather up the kernels and set aside. In a large pan, combine the cobs, onion, carrot, capsicum, garlic, lemongrass, turmeric, ginger, bay leaves and water. Cover and bring to the boil. Remove the lid, then turn down to a slow simmer for 30 minutes. Then add the potato and leave to simmer for another 30 minutes.

Remove the corn cobs, lemongrass and bay leaves, then add the sweetcorn kernels, salt, pepper and chilli powder (if using). Simmer this mixture for 6 minutes. Remove from the heat, cool then blend until smooth. Place a sieve over a clean pan or large jug and push the cooked mixture through, using a ladle or similar. Tip out the roughage and repeat until finished. Put the soup on the heat again, add the cream and season. Stir well and bring to a simmer, then serve with a sprinkle of spring onion.

# Borscht

This beautiful earthy beetroot broth has a delicious sour tang from the addition of vinegar at the end of cooking. But I like to add sauerkraut instead of vinegar (both options are given in the recipe). This nourishing soup from Eastern Europe traditionally uses a beef broth as the stock, but I have substituted dried mushrooms in this recipe. Infusing the dried mushrooms in hot water creates a delicious depth of flavour. Dried porcini mushrooms would be the closest to replicate the ones you would forage in Russia or the Ukraine, but shiitake can also be used. I love the creamy texture of butter beans and they go a beautiful pinkie colour in the soup, but you could also use lentils.

*Vegan | Gluten free*
*Serves 4–6*

6 dried mushrooms, porcini (bolete), morels or shiitake
500ml boiling water
3 tablespoons extra-virgin olive oil
1 tsp caraway seeds
1 red onion, sliced
1 stick celery, sliced
4 beetroot, scrubbed clean and diced into small cubes (if you have the tops, slice finely and stir through the soup at the end with the fresh herbs)
1 carrot, diced into small cubes
1 potato, diced into small cubes
4 cloves garlic, crushed
400g can chopped tomatoes or passata
1.5 litres water
3 bay leaves
400g can butter beans or cooked lentils, drained
1/4 red cabbage, finely sliced
1 tablespoon sweet or hot smoked paprika
1 tsp salt
1/2 tsp cracked black pepper
1–2 tablespoons apple cider vinegar
1/2 cup sauerkraut, red or white
2 tablespoons finely chopped fresh dill, tarragon, parsley or dandelion leaves
1/2 cup sour cream, plant-based or dairy
1 tablespoon fresh horseradish, finely grated or horse radish crème (optional)
Parsley, chopped
2 tablespoons extra-virgin olive oil

Pour the boiling water over the mushrooms to infuse while you prepare the vegetables.

Place a large pot on a high heat and add the olive oil and caraway seeds, then add the onion, celery, beetroot, carrot, potato and garlic. Sauté for 2 minutes.

Remove the mushroom from the soaking water, slice if whole and add to the pot. Stir through and sauté for a further minute. Then add the mushroom soaking liquid along with the tomatoes, water and bay leaves, bring to the boil, then turn down to a simmer and cook for 15 minutes.

Add the beans, red cabbage, paprika, salt and pepper and cook for a further 5 minutes. Add the vinegar and/or a quarter cup of the sauerkraut and herbs and stir through.

Serve each portion with a good dollop of sour cream (with horseradish stirred through), a generous spoonful of sauerkraut, a sprinkle of parsley and a drizzle of extra-virgin olive oil.

PUMPKIN, ZUCCHINI AND / OR SWEETCORN FRITTERS

SPRING RICE ROLLS WITH SATAY SAUCE

SUSHI WITH CRISPY TOFU OR TEMPEH

TOFU MISO BROTH WITH SOBA NOODLES

SOBA NOODLES

ASPARAGUS CRUMBLE

ZUCCHINI CHEESECAKE

BANANA BLOSSOM 'NOT FISHCAKES' WITH AVOCADO MAYO

OKONOMIYAKI

TOFU LAKSA

MISO BAKED AUBERGINE

CAESAR MEETS NIÇOISE SALAD

SPANISH TORTILLA WITH GREEK SALAD

FILO PINWHEELS

FILLED AVOCADOS WITH FENNEL AND SPROUTED MUNGBEAN

FILLED AVOCADOS WITH STRAWBERRY SALSA AND
MACADAMIA

POT STICKER DUMPLINGS

TEMPEH PATTIES, SAUSAGES AND NUGGETS

HOT CHIPS

ROASTED OR BBQ PORTOBELLO MUSHROOMS

# Light Meals

# Pumpkin, Zucchini and/or Sweetcorn Fritters

*Fritters are a 'go to' lunch for me. They are quick to prepare, easy to make and you can use such a myriad of different ingredients for flavouring; they are the perfect versatile lunch. I use a cast-iron pan or a hot plate for fritters. Allow enough room between fritters to flip them easily. Make sure your pan is hot enough to seal the fritters, but not so hot that they burn before the inside is cooked through.*

## Vegan | Gluten free
## Makes 20

4 cups pumpkin, kumara, zucchini, grated (if using zucchini, measure then squeeze out the juice) or 2 cups sweet corn kernels or peas
1 1/2 cups wheat flour
2 tsp baking powder
1 cup cheese, feta or cheddar, plant-based or dairy, crumbled or grated
4 spring onions or onion weed, sliced
1 cup chickpeas (optional)
1/2 cup milk, plant-based or dairy
2 eggs
1/4 cup rice bran or preferred neutral oil

## Gluten-free option
Replace flour with:
1/2 cup chickpea flour
1/2 cup brown rice flour
1 cup potato, corn or tapioca flour

## Vegan option
Replace eggs with:
1/2 cup aquafaba
1/2 tsp cream of tartar

Place prepared vegetables in a bowl along with the flour, baking powder, cheese, spring onion and chickpeas (if using) and milk. Mix well.

Stir in the eggs (or whip the aquafaba with the cream of tartar with an electric whisk for 5 minutes until thick and fluffy).

Heat a frying pan on a medium-high heat and add 2 tablespoons of the oil (use 2 tablespoons per batch). Spoon tablespoons of mixture into the pan, leaving enough room to flip them (five should be about right for your average pan). Flip when bubbles start showing on the top. Make sure the temperature is medium-high so they get a nice colour but also cook through. Flip again when the middle of each fritter is firming up, you should feel a little bounce if you press lightly in the centre. If it's still too soft, flip it again after 30 seconds or so until its cooked. Transfer fritters to a cooling rack.

# Spring Rice Rolls with Satay Sauce

*A perfect lunch in the sun. Fresh, light and delicious, these compact little packages are nutritious and very healthy. I like to get a production line going for rolling the rice rolls so you can roll three at a time.*

*Vegan | Gluten free*

*Makes 15 rolls with 22cm rice paper*

1 clove garlic, crushed
1 tablespoon finely grated ginger
1/4 cup soy sauce, tamari or coconut aminos
1 tsp toasted sesame seed oil
1 block (250g) tempeh, sliced in half lengthways, then into thin pieces
1 bunch asparagus or 6 green beans, tough ends removed and sliced into thirds
1/2 broccoli, finely sliced
1/4 red or green cabbage, finely sliced
1 carrot or fresh mango (skin and pip removed), finely sliced
1 zucchini or 1/2 cucumber (seeds removed by scraping out with a spoon), finely sliced
6 sprigs each of fresh mint and coriander, finely chopped
1/4 cup edible flowers, onion weed, borage, calendula, mizuna (optional)
1 avocado, remove pip, slice carefully in the shell, then squeeze the juice of half a lemon over it and scoop out with a spoon
1/4 cup rice bran oil
1 tablespoon coconut oil
1 tsp toasted sesame seed oil
2 tablespoons sesame seeds
2 tablespoons honey or alternative syrup
2 tablespoons coconut or rice vinegar
juice of 1 lime
2 tablespoons sweet soy sauce (or sweet chilli sauce and tamari soy sauce)

In a large bowl, combine the garlic, ginger, soy sauce, first measure of toasted sesame seed oil and tempeh. Stir carefully with a spatula and leave to marinate while you prepare the vegetables, herbs and edible flowers. Remove tempeh from marinade and set aside.

In a large frying pan or wok, heat the rice bran oil, coconut oil and second measure of toasted sesame seed oil on a medium-high heat. Fry the tempeh for 1 minute on each side. Add the sesame seeds and honey and fry for a further 30 seconds, moving constantly so they don't burn. Transfer from the pan to a plate.

In the same pan, add the asparagus pieces with 1 tablespoon of water and sauté for 1 minute, remove and repeat for the broccoli pieces. Meanwhile, add the remaining vegetables to the leftover marinade along with the coconut or rice vinegar, lime juice, sweet soy sauce (or sweet chilli sauce and tamari).

Add the cooked tempeh, asparagus and broccoli to the bowl and mix well.

Soak rice papers in very hot tap water, one at a time. This is best done in a pan that is large enough to submerge the sheets of paper until they soften. Once softened, lay out each sheet on a clean bench or plate, I do two or three at a time. Place a slice of avocado, edible flowers (if using) and a good pinch of the filling (about 1 heaped tablespoon) strained of excess liquid on the rice paper, and shape it into a log. Fold the back edge of the rice paper over the filling, then fold in each side and roll up.

Transfer the rolls to the plate you will be eating them from; they are a bit sticky and don't like to be moved. Repeat until all the mixture has been used. Serve with Satay Sauce – dip and enjoy.

For a quick satay sauce: add a tin of coconut cream, 1/2 cup peanut butter, 1/4 cup soy sauce, 1/4 cup sweet chilli sauce and 2 tablespoons of tamarind paste to a pot and bring to a simmer, stirring constantly until emulsified. Simmer for 5 minutes to thicken, remove from the heat and serve.

# Sushi with Crispy Tofu or Tempeh

*Vegan | Gluten free*
*Makes 4 rolls or 18 pieces*

1 cup white short-grain sushi rice + 2 cups water
or 1 cup brown sushi rice + 3 cups water
1 tsp salt
2 tablespoons sesame seeds, toasted
2 tablespoons rice or white vinegar
1 tablespoon sugar
4 nori sheets

## Filling Options

Crispy Tofu or Tempeh
1 carrot, sliced lengthways into thin sticks
1 capsicum, cored, deseeded and sliced into thin strips
1 egg omelette, cut in half or into 3 long slices
1 avocado, stone removed and sliced lengthways + the juice of 1 lemon squeezed over
1/2 cucumber, sliced lengthways into quarters
2 lettuce leaves, finely sliced
4 radishes, thinly sliced
1/4 cup Mayonnaise (page 40) or
Avo Mayo (page 114)

## Crispy Tofu or Tempeh

300g firm tofu or tempeh, cut into 0.5cm dice or batons
1/4 cup rice bran or coconut oil
1 tsp toasted sesame oil
1 tablespoon light soy sauce, tamari or coconut aminos

Place the rice, water and salt in a pot, cover and bring to the boil. Stir and turn down to a gentle simmer, cook for 30 minutes for white rice, 40 minutes for brown, stir once during this time. Remove from the heat, stir again, replace the lid and let the rice steam for 10 minutes.

Toast the sesame seeds in a dry pan on a high heat, shaking constantly until starting to colour and pop. Add to the rice along with the vinegar, and sugar, stir through and leave to cool. Tip onto a plate to cool if in a hurry.

Meanwhile, prepare the fillings. If adding the Crispy Tofu or Tempeh to the rice, stir this through the rice when ready and leave to cool all together.

To assemble the sushi, you will need a bowl of cold water to dip your hands in and to secure the roll. Remove the nori sheets from the packet and take 1 cup of cooked, cooled rice and spread it out evenly and carefully over three-quarters of the nori, push it right out to the edges, leaving a strip clear on the long side furthest from you.

Lay the filling in a row on the opposite edge to the clear edge. You only need 1 or 2 rows of filling. Start rolling from the edge with the filling (using a bamboo sushi mat, if you have one), tuck it in while you are rolling it evenly to form a tight roll with the filling in the centre. Dampen your fingers with water and pat over the clear edge of nori, then roll to secure it.

Place on a clean chopping board, sealed-side down, and repeat until the rice is finished. I use a small, serrated knife to slice into about eight pieces per roll. Serve with soy sauce, pickled ginger, wasabi or kimchi.

## Crispy Tofu or Tempeh

In a wok or large frying pan, heat the oils on a high heat. Add the tofu or tempeh pieces to the hot oil, you may like to do this in two batches so to not overcrowd the pan. Cook until coloured before turning.

When all sides are crispy and nicely coloured, transfer from the oil to a separate bowl using a slotted spoon and sprinkle with the soy sauce.

# Tofu Miso Broth with Soba Noodles

*This satisfying meal in a bowl is quick and easy to prepare. The cubes of tofu are like little sponges sucking up the flavours of the soup, which makes them really tasty. They also add texture and protein to this dish. I like to use dried shiitake to make a stock but you could also use fresh, or use both. If you aren't making stock with the mushrooms, you will need to add 800ml water or vegetable stock to the recipe.*

*Vegan | Gluten free*
*Serves 4*

6 dried shiitake mushrooms, rehydrated in 800ml boiling water
1–2 pieces of seaweed, common kelp, wakame, kombu or nori (optional)
200g soba noodles, store-bought or use the recipe on page 108
1 tablespoon toasted sesame oil
3 tablespoons rice bran, peanut or coconut oil
300g tofu, cubed
2 shallots or 1 red onion or 1/2 leek, finely sliced
2–3 cloves garlic, crushed or diced
1 carrot or capsicum, diced
2 sticks celery, thinly sliced
1/4 cup miso paste
1–2 tablespoons finely grated fresh ginger
1 tablespoon finely grated fresh turmeric (optional)
1 tablespoon sweet soy sauce
3 tablespoons light soy sauce, tamari or coconut aminos
2 tablespoons mirin
1/2 broccoli, cut into florets or Asian leafy green, roughly chopped

Soak the mushrooms with the seaweed (if using). Three-quarter fill a big pot with water, put the lid on and bring to the boil. Add the noodles and boil for 1 minute for fresh or to the instructions on the packet, until just cooked. Strain, rinse with cold water or plunge into an ice bowl.

Put a wok or large frying pan on a high heat and add the sesame and rice bran oil. Add the tofu and fry, without moving, for 1 minute. Flip then cook for another minute. Add the shallots, garlic and the prepared vegetables and stir-fry for 1 minute.

Remove the mushrooms from the liquid, squeeze over the jug to remove moisture, slice and add to the wok. Stir-fry for a couple more minutes. Mix a quarter cup of the mushroom stock with the miso paste until smooth and add the rest of the stock to the wok along with the ginger, turmeric, sweet soy sauce, soy sauce and mirin. Simmer for 10 minutes then add the broccoli and cook for 1 minute. Add the miso mix and stir through, switch off the heat.

Place a portion of noodles in each bowl and ladle the broth over the top.

# Soba Noodles

*Fresh homemade soba noodles are super tasty, nutty, savoury, delicate and totally delicious. In Japan there are shops and restaurants completely dedicated to soba noodles, so it must be something we are missing out on! Japanese food has to be one of the best cuisines in the world and making these noodles from scratch at home is really satisfying. These are more delicate than store-bought noodles, especially if using regular buckwheat flour; using a high-gluten wheat flour will help.*

## Vegan | Gluten free
### Serves 4

1 cup buckwheat flour
1/2 cup flour, wholemeal, plain or high grade
3/4 cup (190ml) hot water
1 tsp salt
2 tsp toasted sesame oil
2 tsp peanut or rice bran oil

## Gluten-free option

**Replace flours and water with:**
1 cup buckwheat flour
1/4 cup psyllium husk (mix with 3/4 cup hot water before adding)
1/3 cup tapioca flour, plus 2 tablespoons for dusting the bench if needed

Measure the buckwheat flour, flour and water into a mixing bowl. Stir the mixture with a butter knife until it starts to come together. Tip onto the bench and knead for 5 minutes until smooth and leave to rest under the bowl for 10 minutes.

## To roll by hand:
Dust the bench and rolling pin with flour. Divide the dough into four. Use the rolling pin to roll each piece out to 2mm thick, fold into four and cut into thin strips using a sharp knife (or you could use a pizza cutter) to cut into thin ribbons. Lay noodles on a floured board. Repeat until finished.

## To roll with a pasta machine:
Divide the dough into four then roll each piece to mark 4 with plenty of flour. Then roll through the spaghetti cutter. Repeat until done adding scraps to resting pieces of dough, until all the dough has been used.

## To cook:
Bring a pot with plenty of water to the boil. Add the salt along with the noodles and cook for 1 minute. Remove from the heat and pour through a colander to the remove water. Cool the noodles down with cold running water or plunge into an ice-cold bowl of water. Drain and add toasted sesame oil and peanut or rice bran oil and gently toss through.

Serve with the Tofu Miso Broth or kimchi and crispy tofu or cold dipped in soba sauce.

# Asparagus Crumble

*A savoury crumble might be pretty out there for some, but trust me you will love this recipe. It makes a great side dish in the springtime or you could take your brunch game up a notch and serve it with a couple of poached eggs or tofu scramble.*

Vegan | Gluten free
Serves 4

1 thick slice of bread, wheat or gluten free, torn into small pieces
2 cloves garlic, crushed or roasted
3 tablespoons extra-virgin olive oil
200g feta, plant-based or dairy, crumbled
3 tablespoons pine nuts or pistachios
zest of 1 lemon
1 tsp fresh thyme leaves
1/2 tsp salt
1/4 tsp cracked black pepper
1 bunch asparagus, tough ends snapped off
pinch of salt
2 calendula flowers, petals only (optional)

Preheat the oven to 200°C. Place the bread, garlic, 2 tablespoons of the olive oil, feta, nuts, lemon zest, thyme and seasoning into a bowl. Stir together and set aside.

Pour the final tablespoon of olive oil into an ovenproof dish along with the asparagus and a pinch of salt and roast for 2 minutes. Sprinkle with the topping and the calendula petals (if using) and roast for a further 10–15 minutes until crispy and golden.

# Zucchini Cheesecake

This savoury Zucchini (courgette) Cheesecake recipe is the perfect alternative to a quiche and is a great dish to take to share at a party or picnic. Chargrilling is one of my absolute favourite ways to prepare zucchini, they have a high water content so to achieve good char lines you need to press them down when you put them on the grill and again when you flip them. You will need a stand-alone mixer or handheld electric whisk for the vegetarian version and a food processor for the vegan version of this recipe. The food processor is also used for the base but the seeds could be chopped by hand then mixed together in a mixing bowl before pushing into the tin. I do find the mini food processors great for chopping seeds and nuts to a good consistency, far superior to larger ones. Squeezing out the excess liquid from the zucchini is an essential part of the recipe and I like to place the grater on top of a clean tea towel and grate them straight onto it, then gather the edges together and squeeze the life out of it. After you have squeezed till you can't squeeze any more, leave it sitting in the tea towel until you are ready to use it.

## Vegan | Gluten free
## Makes 25cm cheesecake
## Serves 12

1/2 cup raw walnuts or pumpkin seeds
3/4 cup sunflower seeds
1 cup wholemeal or oat flour
1/2 tsp salt
100g butter, plant-based or dairy, cubed and chilled or refined coconut oil
4 zucchini, 2 grated and squeezed thoroughly to remove excess water and 2 sliced into 4mm thick rounds or on the diagonal if small
2 tablespoons extra-virgin olive oil
1 tablespoon fresh thyme, roughly chopped

### Gluten-free option
Replace wholemeal or oat flour with:
1 cup buckwheat and brown rice flour
2 tablespoons psyllium husk
1 tablespoon ground flaxseed with 1/4 cup water, leave to absorb for 10 minutes before adding

## Vegetarian filling
250g almond ricotta (page 16)
250g cream cheese
6 eggs
4 tsp cornflour
1 tablespoon mustard powder
1/2 cup cream
1 tsp salt
1/4 tsp cracked black pepper

## Vegan Filling
2 x 300g blocks tofu
1 cup pre-soaked cashew nuts
3/4 cup nutritional yeast
1 tablespoon mustard powder
1 tsp baking powder
1 clove garlic, peeled
4 tsp cornflour or tapioca flour
1/2 cup water
1/3 cup extra-virgin olive oil
1 tsp salt
1/4 tsp cracked black pepper
2 tablespoons chopped chives, onion flower stems or coriander
1 tablespoon chopped mint or basil

Line a 25cm springform tin with baking paper.

For the base, measure the walnuts and sunflower seeds into a food processor and blitz until finely chopped, then add the flour, salt and butter. Pulse together until it becomes one mass. Push the dough evenly into the lined tin and refrigerate while you prepare the filling.

Preheat the oven to 150°C. Prepare the zucchini, adding the thyme and olive oil to the sliced pieces. Chargrill the slices on both sides on a smoking hot grill or grill pan and set the grated zucchini aside.

To make the vegetarian filling, measure the ricotta and cream cheese into a large bowl or mixing bowl with a whisk attachment and beat until smooth. Add the eggs and continue beating until light and fluffy, about 5 minutes. Mix the cornflour, mustard powder, cream, salt and black pepper together in a small bowl. Reduce the beater speed, then pour the mixture from the small bowl into the mixer bowl and beat for another 30 seconds.

To make the vegan filling, measure the tofu, cashew nuts, nutritional yeast, mustard powder, baking powder, garlic, cornflour, water, olive oil, salt and pepper into a food processor.

Fold the reserved grated zucchini into the filling mixture along with the herbs. Place the filling on the chilled base, then bake for 1 hour or so; the filling should be set but retain a little wobble. There may be cracks in it but don't worry.

Cool in the tin, then remove the outside ring and chill further in the fridge before sliding it out of the base. Top with the chargrilled zucchini and serve.

# Banana Blossom 'Not Fish Cakes' with Avocado Mayo

*Crispy on the outside, soft in the middle with a distinctive sea taste from the nori, these 'not fish cakes' are the perfect way to utilise banana blossoms which have a flaky fish type consistency once cooked. I love to serve these simply with avocado mayo and fresh bread with sliced cucumber, lettuce or a side salad.*

*The Avocado Mayo is the best! A great way to use slightly over-ripe or ugly avocados and lasts for over a week in the fridge without going brown. The avocado works like egg yolks to thicken the mayo and it tastes delicious. The aquafaba will give the mayo extra stability and shelf-life but is not necessary, it also will fix a split mayo (instructions below). You do need a mini food processor, stick blender or high-speed blender for the best results.*

### Vegan | Gluten free
### Makes 12

1 potato or kumara, cooked and mashed
400g can butter or cannellini beans, drained, reserve the brine (aquafaba)
500g can banana blossoms, drained and torn into rough pieces
7 nori sheets, cut six in half and one torn into bite-sized pieces
6 spring onions or onion weed, finely chopped
zest of 1 lemon
1 tablespoon capers (optional)
1 cup roughly chopped oxalis (optional)
1 tsp salt
1/4 tsp cracked black pepper
1/2 cup potato or cornflour
1 cup breadcrumbs, panko or jasmine rice crumbs
1/2 cup rice bran or coconut oil

### Avocado Mayo (Makes 300ml)
1 avocado, skin and stone removed
2 tablespoons aquafaba (optional)
1 tablespoon stoneground mustard or wasabi
1 clove garlic, peeled
1/2 tsp unrefined sugar
50ml rice bran oil
zest and juice of 1 lemon
1/2 tsp salt
1/4 tsp black pepper

Place the mashed potato and beans in a bowl. Add the banana blossoms, torn nori, spring onion, lemon zest, capers (if using), oxalis (if using), salt and pepper. Stir to combine. Shape into palm-sized cakes and wrap each cake in half a nori sheet and place join-side down to secure. Lightly coat each cake with the potato flour, dip into the aquafaba then into the breadcrumbs. Repeat until all are coated.

Heat 3 tablespoons of oil at a time in a frying pan and fry each side until golden brown, about 4 minutes on each side, adjust the temperature as needed. Transfer from the pan to a cooling rack and repeat until all the cakes are cooked.

Serve with Avocado Mayo, cucumber, lettuce and fresh bread or a side salad.

To make the Avocado Mayo, measure the avocado, aquafaba (if using), mustard, garlic and sugar into a mini food processor and blitz together until smooth. Add the oil 2 tablespoons at a time and blitz well between each addition until thick and smooth. Then add the lemon juice, salt and pepper and blitz together well.

Store in a sealed container or jar in the fridge. If the mayo splits, remove it from the food processor, add 2 tablespoons of the split mixture back to the processor along with 2 tablespoons of aquafaba and process together until emulsified. Continue to add a couple of tablespoons of the split mixture back at a time until all of the mayo is emulsified.

# Okonomiyaki

These Japanese-inspired savoury pancakes are light, crispy and topped with all sorts of little taste explosions. Traditionally made with eggs, cabbage, yams and meaty ingredients, this version is pared back quite a bit and I've deviated from the traditional ingredients, but it definitely doesn't leave you wanting. Japanese Kewpie Mayonnaise, okonomiyaki sauce, thinly sliced nori sheets and pickles are generally the main accompaniments, you could also tear up a piece of nori and add it to the pancake mix to add the sea flavour. I like to use hemp seed oil for frying as it imparts a slightly fishy taste when heated also which makes up for not using katsuobushi (bonito flakes). Cooked taro is a great substitute for the traditional Japanese nagaimo (yam) but is not essential. Using a cast-iron pan is the best for okonomiyaki and I like to utilise my little 12cm pans for individual portions but you could also make bigger ones and cut them into pieces instead.

## Vegan | Gluten free
### Makes 4 x 12cm pan-sized servings

1/2 cup sliced spring onions or onion weed
1/2 cup finely sliced white cabbage
1/2 cup grated nagaimo or cooked taro (optional)
1 block tofu (300g), drained and crumbled
1 tablespoon grated fresh ginger
1 tsp salt
6 eggs
1/4 cup flour
1/4 cup hemp seed or rice bran oil
1 tsp toasted sesame oil
1–2 nori sheets, cut in half and thinly sliced
1–2 tablespoons gomashio (black and white sesame seeds, kelp and salt)
1/4 cup Japanese pickles, kimchi or pickled ginger

## Gluten-free | Vegan option

Replace the eggs and flour with:
200ml aquafaba
1/2 tsp cream of tartar
3 tablespoons chickpea flour
3 tablespoons brown rice flour
3 tablespoons tapioca starch

## Okonomiyaki Sauce

1/2 cup light soy sauce, tamari or coconut aminos
2–3 tablespoons coconut sugar, honey or maple syrup
1–2 tablespoons tomato paste or puree
2 tablespoons grated fresh ginger
3 cloves garlic, crushed
2 tsp smoke liquid
1 tsp toasted sesame oil
3 tablespoons mirin
1 tablespoon cornflour mixed with 1/4 cup water

Place the spring onions, cabbage, yam, tofu, ginger and salt in a bowl and stir to combine. Add the eggs and flour and stir through (or whisk the aquafaba with the cream of tartar with an electric whisk for 5 minutes until thick and fluffy. Add the chickpea flour, brown rice flour and tapioca starch to the bowl along with the fluffy aquafaba and fold through.)

Mix the two oils together and heat 2 tablespoons at a time in a frying pan on a high heat. Spoon about a quarter of the mix into the pan and turn down the temperature to a medium-high heat. Cook on each side until golden brown. Time depends on whether you are using eggs or not but about 1–2 minutes each side. Transfer the pancakes from the pan to a plate or cooling rack and repeat until all the mixture has been used.

Spread or zigzag the sauces on and sprinkle with nori and gomashio.

To make the Okonomiyaki Sauce, measure all the ingredients, apart from the cornflour mix, into a pot. Bring to a simmer and cook for 5 minutes, stirring occasionally. Add the cornflour mix while stirring and cook for a further minute. Remove from the heat and pour into a warm, sterilised bottle and cap. Keep in the fridge once opened.

# Tofu Laksa

*Laksa is one of my all-time favourite meals, noodles swimming in an unctuous, spicy, aromatic soup base topped with crispy tofu and fresh herbs, heaven in a bowl for Southeast Asian food lovers.*

### Vegan | Gluten free
### Serves 4

1 aubergine, cut into cubes
1 tablespoon salt
1/4 cup coconut or rice bran oil
1 block (300g) firm tofu, diced into 1cm pieces
1 tablespoon light soy sauce, tamari or coconut aminos
1 onion, sliced
1 stick celery, sliced
1 carrot or capsicum, sliced
2 tablespoons mirin
400ml can coconut cream, rinsed with 400ml water
1 litre vegetable stock or 1 litre water + 1 tsp vegetable stock powder
1 piece of kombu, kelp or a nori sheet (optional)
3 tomatoes, grated to remove skin
3 kaffir lime leaves or the zest and juice of 1 lime
1/4 cup tamarind paste
1/4 cup light soy sauce, tamari or coconut aminos
300g dry udon or thick rice noodles
1 tablespoon rice bran or other neutral oil
8 fresh green or yellow beans, sliced
2 spring onions or onion weed, sliced
1/2 cup mung bean sprouts (optional)
2–4 whole fresh coriander sprigs, finely chop the roots and stems and roughly chop the leaves just before using

### Laksa Paste

2 shallots, peeled
4 cloves garlic, peeled
2–3 whole red chillies or 1 red capsicum, cored and deseeded
1 tablespoon ground coriander
2 tsp ground cumin
1 thumb-sized piece ginger, roughly chopped
1 thumb-sized piece turmeric, roughly chopped
2 stalks lemongrass, tough outer leaves removed and finely sliced

Measure all the paste ingredients into a food processor and blitz until smooth.

Place the aubergine in a colander, sprinkle with salt and leave to drain while you prepare the laksa paste.

Heat the coconut oil in a wok or large frying pan on a high heat. When the coconut oil has melted, add the tofu and cook without moving too often until crispy, this will take about 10 minutes. Use a slotted spoon to transfer the tofu from the wok to a bowl, toss through the first measure of soy sauce and set aside.

Add the onion, celery and carrot to the wok. Pat the aubergine dry with a clean tea towel or similar and add to the wok also. Stir-fry for 2 minutes. Add the laksa paste and fry, constantly moving, for another 2 minutes. Then add the mirin, coconut cream, vegetable stock, seaweed, tomato pulp, lime leaves, tamarind paste and soy sauce. Bring to the boil, then turn down and simmer for 20 minutes.

Put another pan of water on to boil. If using rice noodles, pour the boiled water over the noodles and leave to sit for 10 minutes, stirring occasionally to cook evenly. If using udon noodles, add them to the boiling water. Stir the noodles with a fork to ensure even cooking and boil for 8 minutes or until cooked. Strain in a colander and rinse and sit them in cold water until ready to add to soup, drain again and toss together with the rice bran oil so they don't stick together.

Add the tofu to the soup and the beans and simmer for one more minute. Place the noodles in serving bowls, then add the soup and top with the spring onions, bean sprouts and coriander leaves.

# Miso Baked Aubergine

*These deliciously unctuous melt-in-the-mouth aubergine halves are an absolute must for aubergine lovers. Perfectly grilled and singing with Asian flavours they would pair perfectly with soba noodles and chilli oil, tempeh nuggets and rice, stir fried greens or topped with crispy lentils and served with roasted kumara.*

*Vegan | Gluten free*
*Serves 4*

2 aubergines, sliced in half lengthways and flesh scored in a criss-cross pattern
1 tsp salt
1 tablespoon miso paste
2 tablespoons hot water
1 tablespoon mirin
1 tablespoon peanut or rice bran oil
1/4 tsp sesame oil
1 clove garlic, crushed
1 tablespoon finely grated ginger
1 tablespoon light soy sauce, tamari or coconut aminos
1 tablespoon peanut butter
2 tablespoons rice bran oil
1 tsp sesame seeds

Place the aubergine in a colander, sprinkle the cut sides with salt and leave to drain while you prepare the glaze. Preheat the oven to 190°C.

Measure the miso paste, hot water, mirin, oils, garlic, ginger, soy sauce and peanut butter into a bowl. Mix well and set aside.

Heat the rice bran oil in a cast-iron pan or hotplate on a high heat. Pat the aubergine dry and place it cut side down into the heated pan. Adjust to a medium-high heat fry aubergine for 3 minutes, turn, they should be golden brown. Cook for a further 3 minutes then transfer to an ovenproof dish with a lid.

Spread the prepared miso mixture onto the aubergine and sprinkle with the sesame seeds. Cover and cook at 180°C for 20 minutes.

Serve as a side dish or as a meal with steamed brown rice and Tempeh Nuggets (page 132).

# Caesar Meets Niçoise Salad

*This salad has all the favourites and is a meal in a bowl. It would work equally well for a lunch or salad to have at a barbeque. Peruperu potatoes are perfect for this salad, little waxy gems, however any new season waxy type potato will do. There are sprouted pulses in this recipe to prepare in advance. Soak dried pulses overnight covered, drain next morning through a sieve, then leave in sieve and cover with a tea towel. Rinse the beans again that night, then again next morning until they sprout. They are now ready to use. Also there are options for the bacon element.*

### Vegan | Gluten free
### Serves 4-6

6 eggs, boiled, cooled and peeled or 1 avocado, halved and quartered + juice of 1 lemon squeezed over

8 small potatoes, scrubbed and steamed until tender

1 bunch asparagus or green beans, tough ends removed

2 tablespoons extra-virgin olive oil

1/2 tsp salt

1/2 cup mixed pulse sprouts: chickpea, mung bean and/or lentil

1 radicchio, cos or romaine lettuce, rinsed and roughly chopped

4 tomatoes, quartered and sliced or 8 cherry tomatoes, halved

10 olives, pitted

200g plant-based bacon fried until crispy or a Smoky Substitute (page 30)

2 thick slices bread, wheat or gluten free, each cut into four

1 tablespoon chopped fresh thyme or rosemary leaves

1/4 cup extra-virgin olive oil

2 spring onions or 8 onion weed including flowers, finely sliced

a few grinds of salt and black pepper

1/3 cup Mayonnaise (page 40) or Yoghurt Dressing (page 42)

1/3 cup parmesan, shaved or Hemp Parmesan (page 22)

a handful of edible flowers, e.g. nasturtium, borage, pansy or calendula (optional)

Load up your steamer with eggs for boiling in the bottom, potatoes in the first layer and asparagus or beans in the top layer. Steam the asparagus or beans for 2 minutes then run under cold water to cool quickly and retain colour, leave to drain.

When the potatoes are done, tip out onto a serving platter or bowl to cool and drizzle over the first measure of olive oil and salt. Continue preparing the rest of the ingredients, then add to the bowl or platter as you go.

When the eggs are boiled, slice the whites and leave the yolks whole, add to bowl. Fry the plant-based bacon in rice bran oil until crispy. Chop and add to bowl. Fry the bread with the olive oil and rosemary until golden.

Season and dress the salad with your choice of dressing and toss together well. Top with freshly shaved parmesan or hemp parmesan and edible flowers, if you have them.

# Spanish Tortilla with Greek Salad

*I lived off this dish in Spain along with bread and olive oil. It is essentially a potato omelette, similar to an Italian frittata. Great hot or cold for a picnic, it has very few ingredients and is plain enough for the kids to enjoy. Our local peruperu potatoes are perfect for this dish as they are a waxy variety. I find a cast-iron pan the best for making this dish and, when cutting the potatoes, I find slicing them into different shapes works the best.*

*Vegan | Gluten free*

*Serves 4*

*Makes a 20cm round tortilla*

1/2 cup extra-virgin olive oil
1 onion, finely sliced
3 waxy potatoes, finely sliced
6 eggs
1 tsp salt

*Greek Salad*

1 red onion, finely sliced
2 tablespoons red wine vinegar
6–8 tomatoes, roughly cut
1 tsp dried oregano
1/2 tsp cracked black pepper
1 cucumber, cut into chunks
1/2 cup Kalamata olives, pitted if preferred
200g block Greek-style feta, salty goat or sheep milk feta or casheta
1/4 cup extra-virgin olive oil
salt to taste
a few leaves of fresh basil, mint or parsley

*Vegan Option*

Replace eggs with:
1 cup chickpea flour + 1 cup aquafaba +1 tsp white vinegar, whisked together

Heat the olive oil in a cast-iron pan on a medium heat. Add the onion and potatoes and sauté for 10 minutes, moving often.

Break the eggs into a bowl and stir with a fork to break up. Using a slotted spoon, remove the onions and potatoes from the pan and place in the bowl. Add the salt, stir and leave to sit, covered for 15 minutes.

Heat the olive oil left in the pan on a medium-high heat and pour the thickened mixture into the pan. Fry for 2 minutes, then reduce to a medium heat and cook for a further 5 minutes. Run a bread and butter knife around the sides, then put a plate on top, hold it firmly and then confidently flip the omelette over onto the plate. Put the pan back on the heat and gently push the omelette back into the pan and cook the other side for a further 3 minutes.

To remove from the pan, place the plate back on top and flip it over. Serve with a Greek salad or the Gazpacho (page 92).

To make the Greek Salad, prepare the ingredients straight into a salad bowl. Serve without tossing together is the traditional way.

# Filo Pinwheels

*These quick, easy pinwheels are like little pinwheel pies and are great for when you have a few people over, to take to a pot-luck dinner or as an easy-to-eat lunch or picnic. This took me 30 minutes to prep from start to finish and can be adapted for vegans or made a little cheesy. It is great both ways, so grab your trusty pastry brush and let's get started.*

## Vegan
## Makes 24 pinwheels

8 cups roughly chopped silverbeet, kale or spinach
1/2 tsp salt
1 cup water
2 zucchini, grated
3 cloves garlic, crushed
zest of 1 lemon
1/2 cup pitted olives, roughly chopped
3 sprigs dill or fennel, finely chopped
2 sprigs mint, finely chopped
1/2 cup parsley or coriander, finely chopped
250g Almond Ricotta (page 16), Dairy Ricotta (page 21) or tofu, crumbled
250g cream cheese, plant-based or dairy, grated
1 tsp salt
1/2 tsp cracked black pepper
375g packet of filo
1 egg (or 1 tablespoon chia seeds + 3 tablespoons water - leave to absorb for 10 minutes)
100g butter, plant-based or dairy, melted or 100ml extra-virgin olive oil
2 tablespoons sesame seeds
1 cup cherry tomatoes, whole

Place the prepared greens, salt and water in a pan, cover with the lid and cook on high heat for 5 minutes until just wilted (turn once during this time to ensure even cooking). Remove from the heat and tip into a colander then run under cold water to cool quickly. Squeeze well to remove as much water as you can, then place in a clean, dry tea towel.

Meanwhile, squeeze the excess liquid from the grated zucchini, then place in the tea towel with the silverbeet. Fold the tea towel over the silverbeet and zucchini and twist the ends in opposite directions to squeeze out all the excess liquid.

Preheat the oven to 190°C. Place the greens in a bowl followed by the garlic, lemon zest, olives, herbs, cheeses, seasoning and egg. Stir together well.

Line a baking tray with baking paper. Place three sheets of filo together and butter the top layer using a pastry brush. Place another three sheets halfway along the first lot and again butter the top layer. Repeat twice more to form an 80cm length of filo.

Butter the entire length, then place one sheet across each join. Butter the entire length again. At this point you should have four sheets of filo left. Distribute the filling evenly over the filo leaving 3cm at each end and along the furthest edge from you (top edge). Fold the side edges in over the filling. Butter the folded in edges and, starting at the side closest to you, roll up like a pinwheel, tucking it under itself, starting from one end gradually tucking and rolling from end to end.

Line up the remaining filo sheets directly in front of you, the roll should now be at arms-length. Butter the extra sheets to join them together, if needed. Then butter this all over and roll the sausage back over it towards you. This will hold it all together.

Using a serrated knife, cut the sausage in half, then each piece in half again, then each piece in half again, until you have eight equal pieces. Now cut each piece into three so in total you should have 24 pinwheels. Turn them on their cut ends and arrange on the baking tray. Brush the tops with butter and sprinkle the sesame seeds evenly over the top. Bake for 30 minutes until golden brown. For a simple garnish, scatter cherry tomatoes over the pinwheels.

# Filled Avocados with Fennel and Sprouted Mung Bean

*These filled avocados are crunchy, creamy, zesty, nutty and nutritious. To make the sprouts, cover dried mung beans with water and leave overnight. Drain through a sieve in the morning. Cover the sieve with a tea towel and rinse the beans again at night then again in the morning until little tails sprout out. They are now ready to use.*

*Vegan | Gluten free*

*Serves 4-6*

1/2 red onion, thinly sliced
1 bulb fennel, very finely sliced (use a mandolin, if you have one)
1 orange or tangelo, peeled and diced
juice of 1 lime
2 tsp clover honey or alternative sweetener
1 tablespoon chia seeds
1 cup mung bean sprouts
a handful of fresh coriander and fennel tops, finely chopped
1 tablespoon extra-virgin olive oil
1/2 tsp salt
a few grinds of black pepper
40g pistachio nuts, shelled
4 avocados

Mix together the onion, fennel, orange, lime, honey, chia seeds, sprouts, herbs, oil, salt and pepper. Leave to marinate for 30 minutes.

Allow one avocado half per person. Cut each avocado in half lengthways and twist it apart. Remove the stone and squeeze some lemon juice over each half. Slice a little flat side on the outside curve so the avocado is stable on the plate.

Add the pistachio nuts to the filling, stir through, and spoon carefully into the pip holes of the avocados. Serve on a bed of rocket, baby spinach or salad greens from your garden.

# Filled Avocados with Strawberry Salsa and Macadamia

*Strawberry salsa may sound a bit weird but it really is a taste sensation! The tangy sweet balsamic reduction makes the strawberries sing, paired with the creamy avocado and crunchy macadamia nuts this dish delights all the senses.*

## Vegan | Gluten free
## Serves 4-6

1/2 red onion, finely diced
2 tablespoons Balsamic Reduction (page 39)
1/2 tsp Himalayan salt
a few grinds of black pepper
10 strawberries, finely diced
1 sprig fresh mint, finely chopped
2 sprigs basil, finely chopped
1/3 cup macadamia nuts, finely chopped (save half to add to the top)
4 avocados, remove the stone and skin carefully
juice of 1 lemon
borage flowers to garnish (optional)

Place the red onion, balsamic reduction, salt and pepper in a bowl. Mix and leave to marinate for 10 minutes. Add the strawberries, herbs, and half the macadamia nuts and gently stir through.

Allow one avocado half per person. Cut each avocado in half lengthways and twist it apart. Remove the stone and squeeze some lemon juice over each half. Slice a little flat side on the outside curve so the avocado is stable on the plate. Spoon the filling carefully into the pip holes of the avocados. Sprinkle the reserved macadamias over the top.

Serve on a bed of rocket, baby spinach or salad greens from your garden and garnish with edible flowers or some smaller basil leaves and drizzle with olive oil.

# Pot Sticker Dumplings

*Crispy on the bottom with a smooth steamed top, dumplings are so delicious it's hard to stop eating them. Luckily this recipe makes enough for a family banquet. Making dumplings is a lovely thing to do as a family or with a group of friends, especially if you are making them from scratch, as it is time consuming to do on your own. This filling recipe is enough for two meals, so freeze the other half for a rainy day. Note that the filling needs to be cut finely so it is easy to fill the dumplings. The dough is soft, so if using a pasta machine you will need gentle hands. The gluten-free wrappers are too fragile for the pasta machine so will need to be done by hand. To freeze the wrappers ensure you place each wrapper between sheets of baking paper.*

## Vegan | Gluten free
## Makes 32-40 dumplings

### Filling
1/4 cup rice bran or peanut oil
1/4 tsp toasted sesame oil
1 onion or leek, diced
1 carrot, diced
1 stalk celery, finely sliced
4 dried shitake mushrooms, soaked in 125ml boiling water
300g block tofu, mashed
300g block tempeh, grated
2 cloves garlic, crushed
2 tablespoons finely grated fresh ginger
3 tablespoons Chinese cooking wine
1 cob sweetcorn, kernels only
8 green beans, finely sliced
1/4 cup light soy sauce, tamari or coconut aminos
1 tablespoon miso paste

### Wrappers
1 cup white flour
1 cup wholemeal flour
1/4 tsp salt
3/4 cup hot water
1/4 cup cold water

### Gluten-free Wrappers
1/3 cup psyllium husk
3/4 cup hot water
1 cup buckwheat or sorghum flour
1/2 cup tapioca flour
1/4 tsp salt

### To Cook
1/2 cup rice bran oil
2 cups water

### Dipping Sauce
1 tablespoon light soy sauce, tamari or coconut aminos
1 tablespoon hot or sweet chilli sauce
1/2 tsp toasted sesame oil
juice of 1 lime

To make the filling, put a wok or similar on a high heat and add the rice bran and sesame oil followed by the onion, carrot and celery. Stir-fry for 2 minutes.

Remove the shiitake mushrooms from the water, slice and add to the wok along with the tofu, tempeh, garlic and ginger. Stir-fry for 5 minutes then add the cooking wine, sweetcorn kernels, green beans and soy sauce and cook for a further 2 minutes. Stir the miso into the shiitake liquid until smooth and add to the wok. Stir through then remove from the heat and set aside to cool.

To make the wrappers, measure the flours, salt and water into a mixing bowl and stir with a butter knife until it starts to come together in one mass. Tip onto the bench and knead for 5 minutes until smooth and leave to rest under the bowl for 30 minutes.

To make the gluten-free wrappers, measure the psyllium and hot water into a mixing bowl and stir together with a butter knife then add the flours and salt and stir with a butter knife until it starts to come together in one mass.

To roll the wrappers by hand, dust the bench and rolling pin with flour. Divide the dough into two and roll each half into a sausage, then cut into 30 pieces. Use

a rolling pin to roll each one out to 2mm thick and trim with a 9.5cm round cutter. Cover the dough and the wrappers with a lightly damp tea towel.

To roll the wrappers with a pasta machine, divide the dough into quarters and roll each piece to mark 4 or 5 with plenty of flour. Use a 9.5 cm round cutter to cut lengths into rounds. Repeat until done adding scraps to resting pieces of dough, until all the dough is used.

Working with one wrapper at a time, place 1 teaspoon of filling into the centre. Brush the edge of one half of the wrapper with water and pick it up off the counter to fold. Fold four or five pleats using your free hand and stick to the dampened edge as you go. Repeat for all.

Place filled dumplings on a floured-dusted large plate or board, covered with a damp tea towel.

Heat 3 tablespoons of oil (for each batch) in a cast-iron pan on a medium-high heat. Add 8–10 dumplings to the pan at a time, placing each one on its flat side. Fry for 1 minute, then add a quarter cup of water and quickly cover the pan with a lid and steam until the water has evaporated and the bases are golden brown and crispy. Remove the dumplings from the pan and place on a cooling rack. Repeat for the rest of the dumplings.

To make the dipping sauce, combine the soy sauce, chilli sauce, sesame oil and lime juice together in a dipping bowl.

# Tempeh Patties, Sausages and Nuggets

This recipe is really versatile: you have two flavouring options plus the mix can be made into patties, nuggets or even sausages. Tempeh is fermented soybeans pressed into a block; it is a pre and probiotic, has a high protein and iron content. What's more it has a delicious umami flavour and robust texture. I am a big advocate for wholefoods and as a lot of plant-protein substitutes are quite highly processed, I love to be able to make my own with only a few wholesome ingredients.

## Vegan | Gluten free
### Makes 4–6 patties or sausages or 12 nuggets

2 eggs, whisked or 2 tablespoons ground flaxseed mixed with 1/3 cup water
250g block tempeh, grated
2 tablespoons brown rice flour
1/2 tsp salt
1/4 tsp pepper
1/4 cup rice bran oil for frying
1/2 tsp sesame oil (for Asian-style patties)

### Asian Style
2 tablespoons sesame seeds, black or white
1 tablespoon light soy sauce, tamari or coconut aminos
1 spring onion or 2 onion weed, finely sliced
1 tablespoon finely grated ginger
1 clove garlic, crushed

### Mediterranean Style
6 sundried tomatoes, diced
1 clove garlic, crushed
2 sprigs sage or oregano, roughly chopped
1 sprig rosemary, roughly chopped

Place the eggs, tempeh, brown rice flour, salt, pepper and flavouring of choice into a bowl and mix well. Shape the mix into patties or nuggets by scooping (3–4 tablespoons for patties or 1 tablespoon for nuggets) up with a spoon and then rolling and pushing into a flattish round patty or press and roll into sausages with your hands.

Heat 2 tablespoons of oil at a time in a frying pan and fry the patties, sausages or nuggets until golden on each side.

# Hot Chips

This recipe is quick, easy and makes crisp delicious hot chips. The key is to heat the oil in the tray while the oven is heating up, so you add the prepared potato to hot oil. Dusting with flour helps with getting a crispy end result, as does cutting the potatoes into thin chips. It will work equally well for wedges but they will need a slightly longer cooking time. Kumara does cook faster than potatoes and tends to burn more easily, so cut them slightly bigger if you are combining and let the potatoes get the full force of the heat by being a little tactical with positioning.

Vegan | Gluten free
Serves 4-6

3 tablespoons rice bran oil
4 large potatoes or kumara, scrubbed clean and cut into about 5mm width chips
2 tablespoons flour or cornflour
1 tablespoon chopped rosemary, thyme, sage or smoked paprika
1/2 tsp salt
1/4 tsp black pepper

Measure the oil into a roasting tray. Place the tray in the oven and preheat to 220°C.

Meanwhile, place the potatoes, flour, rosemary, salt and pepper in a mixing bowl. Toss together well and place carefully in the hot oil in the roasting tray. Bake for 35 minutes, turning two or three times during cooking.

# Roasted or Barbequed Portobello Mushrooms

Mushrooms are a great source of B vitamins, especially riboflavin (B2) which is good for red blood cells. New research shows a mushroom a day is good for protecting against breast cancer, making mushrooms a fantastic addition to everybody's diet. Great in a burger or as a side dish, I also like to make a whole lot of these mushrooms at once so I can have them on hand to add to an antipasto platter, a pasta salad and I've even been known to have a toasted sandwich with marmite, peanut butter, sliced tomato, wilted spinach and a roasted mushroom for breakfast.

Vegan | Gluten free
Makes 8

8 large portobello mushrooms
2 tablespoons butter, plant-based or dairy
3 tablespoons extra-virgin olive oil
2 tablespoons balsamic vinegar or Balsamic Reduction (page 39)
1 tablespoon water
1 sprig rosemary, leaves roughly chopped
2 cloves garlic, peeled and sliced
1/2 tsp salt
1/4 tsp cracked black pepper

Preheat the oven to 180°C. Place the mushrooms, gill-side up, onto a roasting tray lined with baking paper. Place a knob of butter in each mushroom then drizzle with the olive oil, balsamic vinegar, water then sprinkle with rosemary, garlic, salt and pepper.

Cover the tray securely with tin foil lined with baking paper or a lid and bake for 25 minutes.

Alternatively, add the mushrooms to a bowl with all the other ingredients, toss together and cook, gill-side down first, on a barbeque hotplate.

BEETROOT RISOTTO

COTTAGE PIE

MEXICAN COMIDA - MEXICAN MOLE JACKFRUIT
CAULIFLOWER POPCORN - GUACAMOLE
RICE 'N' BEANS - PEPITAS

VEGGIE BURGERS

SUMMER CURRY WITH ONION KULCHA

RAGU WITH POTATO AU GRATIN

ROAST VEGETABLES WITH CRISPY CHICKPEAS,
ROASTED NUTS AND TAHINI MAYO

RATATOUILLE

STUFFING STUFFED VEGETABLES, HASSELBACK POTATOES, ALE
AND MISO GRAVY, YORKIES AND GARLIC BUTTER BEANS

PENNE 'N' CHEESE

SPAGHETTI BOLOGNESE WITH CHARGRILLED BROCCOLI

KUMARA, CASHEW AND CAULIFLOWER CURRY - KASHMIRI RICE

LASAGNE

FIVE-SPICE FRIED RICE

GNOCCHI WITH SUNSHINE SAUCE AND PISTACHIOS

PAD THAI

MUSHROOM STROGANOFF WITH KASHA

BAKED BEANS WITH POLENTA AND AVOCADO SALSA

# Mains

# Beetroot Risotto

*This pretty pink risotto is a great one-pot meal for a weeknight when time is tight. It is definitely one of my 'go to' easy dinner options as it's super versatile flavour-wise. Grating the beetroot and pumpkin makes them melt into the dish while cooking and the pumpkin gives a lovely creamy quality to the risotto. Constant stirring is the key to getting a really creamy risotto, as it releases the starch from the rice. Other flavour options: add a bottle of tomato passata to the mix instead of the beetroot and pumpkin, or add sweetcorn kernels or asparagus towards the end of the cooking time.*

## Vegan | Gluten free
## Serves 4-6

2 tablespoons extra-virgin olive oil (or 1/4 cup if omitting butter)
2 tablespoons butter, plant-based or dairy
2 shallots or 1 red onion, finely sliced
2 cloves garlic, crushed
2 sticks celery, sliced
1 sprig fresh rosemary, oregano and/or thyme, leaves roughly chopped
1 1/2 cups (300g) risotto rice (arborio)
100ml marsala or white wine (optional)
1/4 pumpkin, skin and seeds removed, grated
2 beetroot, scrubbed and grated, save the leafy tops, if possible
1.2 litres hot water, whey or liquid vegetable stock
1 tsp vegetable bouillon powder (omit powder if using liquid stock)
400g can cannellini or butter beans, drained and rinsed (optional)
1/4 cup olives, pitted
1/2 cup roughly chopped fresh parsley
1/2 cup grated tasty cheese or vegan alternative
1/2 cup parmesan or a plant-based alternative, grated (save some for serving)
1 tsp salt
1/2 tsp cracked black pepper

Heat the olive oil and butter in a large pot. When the butter has melted, add the shallot, garlic, celery and herbs. Fry for a couple of minutes, then add the rice and continue to fry until the grains are coated and toasted.

Add the marsala (if using) and stir through, then add the pumpkin and beetroot.

Begin adding the stock to the rice, half a cup at a time, constantly stirring. Add the beans (if using) and olives after the third addition of stock. Test to see if the rice is done; it should be just cooked with a little bite. Add the parsley, cheeses, salt and pepper and stir through.

Serve with a salad of beetroot tops and rocket leaves drizzled with Balsamic Reduction (page 39), extra-virgin olive oil, salt and pepper.

# Cottage Pie

*Comfort food at its best. This wholesome, warming cottage pie is packed with plant proteins nestled in a rich tomato sauce. The creamy, fluffy mash top is achieved by baking the potatoes whole, then scooping out the tender insides. We then turn these into crispy potato skins which are everyone's favourite and make the absolute most of your potatoes. For the best crispy skins buy unwashed potatoes for the best results. For the gluten-free version, use buckwheat groats instead of pearled barley.*

## Vegan | Gluten free
## Serves 6-8

1/4 cup pearl barley or buckwheat groats
1/4 cup brown lentils
1.5 kg potatoes, unwashed agria or other floury potatoes
3 tablespoons extra-virgin olive oil
1 onion, diced
2 sticks celery, finely sliced
4 mushrooms, grated
1 small beetroot or carrot, grated
3 sundried tomatoes in oil, roughly chopped
3 cloves garlic, crushed
1 tablespoon balsamic vinegar
300ml jar passata
1 tablespoon finely chopped fresh sage, or dried
1 tablespoon finely chopped fresh thyme and/or rosemary, or dried
1 tablespoon smoked paprika
1 tablespoon cacao powder
1 tablespoon coconut sugar or brown sugar (optional)
1/4 cup red split lentils
1/2 cup roughly chopped walnuts, Brazil nuts, sunflower seeds or pumpkin seeds
1.2 litres water
1 tsp salt
1 tsp black pepper
2 tablespoons (30g) butter, plant-based or dairy
1/4 cup milk, plant-based or dairy
1 tsp salt
1/2 tsp black pepper
2 tablespoons extra-virgin olive oil

Measure the barley (or buckwheat groats) and the brown lentils into a jug and cover well with hot tap water and leave to soak while you prepare the vegetables. Preheat the oven to 180°C.

Scrub the potatoes, prick with a knife or fork and bake for 45 minutes to 1 hour, until a knife goes all the way through easily.

Heat the olive oil in a pot on a medium-high heat and add the onion, celery, mushroom, beetroot, sundried tomatoes and garlic. Sauté for 5 minutes, then add the balsamic vinegar and stir through. Add the passata, herbs, smoked paprika, cacao, sugar (if using), red lentils and nuts. Drain the barley and brown lentils and add along with the fresh water, cover and simmer for 45 minutes, stirring occasionally. Season with the first measure of salt and pepper and pour into an ovenproof dish.

When the potatoes are ready, remove from the oven, cool for a couple of minutes, slice in half length-ways and scoop the potato flesh into a ricer or bowl, press through or mash together with the butter, milk, and second measure of salt and pepper. Whip together with a fork. Spoon potato on top of the filling then, using a fork, spread it evenly right to the edges. Drizzle with a little olive oil and bake for 45 minutes until golden and bubbly.

Put the leftover potato skins into a roasting tray and drizzle with olive oil and some roughly chopped rosemary, salt and pepper and add to the oven for the last 15 minutes.

Serve with Asparagus Crumble (page 111).

# Mexican Comida

We love Mexican inspired meals and they are great crowd pleasers. Feel free to mix and match the recipes in this feast either as fillings for tacos, to top nachos, or take as a potluck contribution to a Mexican meal with friends. The mole is a versatile recipe that can be made with pulled wheat meat, plant-based mince, jackfruit or lentils or a mixture, and is perfect for filling soft tacos. Rice and beans are a perfect protein hit, as the combination makes it a complete protein. Complete proteins are what our bodies need every day to stay healthy. This combination contains all the essential amino acids our body doesn't make on its own. You can start this off on the stove top if your ovenproof dish allows. I like to soak the brown rice while I'm preparing the ingredients as it shortens the cooking time. The cauliflower popcorn is a play on Mexican's love of corn and fried chicken. These little crispy bites are healthy, crunchy on the outside, tender on the inside and are a perfect accompaniment to a Mexican meal. My version of guacamole keeps it simple and I love to have my jalapeno fix incorporated into the mix. Toasted pumpkin seeds are not only tasty they add a nice crunch to the meal. They are nutrient rich, high in protein and dietary fibre so scatter them liberally over your meal and enjoy.

## Mexican Mole Jackfruit

*Vegan | Gluten free*
*Makes 6 servings*

1/4 cup extra-virgin olive oil
1 red onion, diced
1/2 red capsicum, deseeded and finely chopped
2 cloves garlic, crushed
2 tablespoons ground cumin
1 tablespoon ground coriander
300g pulled wheat meat, plant-based mince or cooked lentils
400g can jackfruit, drained and roughly broken up
2 tablespoons smoked paprika
100ml water or broth from the wheat meat
400ml tomato passata
2 chipotle peppers in adobo sauce (optional)
1 tablespoon raw cacao powder
1 tablespoon molasses or agave syrup
1 tablespoon coconut sugar (optional)
1 tablespoon dried or chopped fresh oregano
1/2 tsp salt
1/2 tsp black pepper
juice of 1 lime

Heat the olive oil in a pan on high heat. Add the onion and capsicum and fry for 2 minutes.

Add the garlic, spices, your choice of protein, jackfruit, paprika, water, passata, chipotle peppers (if using), cacao powder, molasses, coconut sugar (if using), oregano, salt and pepper. Cook for 10 minutes, remove from the heat and finish with lime juice.

# Cauliflower Popcorn

*Vegan | Gluten free*
*Serves 4-6*

1/2 cup panko, jasmine rice crumbs or crushed cornflakes
1/4 cup fine polenta
1/4 cup cornmeal flour
2 tsp dried oregano
2 tsp sweet smoked paprika
1 tsp garlic powder or 1 clove garlic, crushed
1 tsp black pepper
2 tsp white pepper
1 tsp mustard
1/2 tsp salt
2 tablespoons refined coconut oil, or extra-virgin olive oil
2 tablespoons smooth peanut butter or cashew butter
1 tablespoon maple syrup
2 tablespoons light soy sauce, tamari or coconut aminos
2 tsp hot sauce or tomato sauce
1 cauliflower, cut into small florets

Preheat the oven to 200°C.

Mix the panko, polenta, cornmeal flour, oregano, paprika, garlic, peppers, mustard and salt together in a bowl.

Place the oil, nut butter, maple syrup, soy sauce and hot sauce in a pot and heat while whisking continuously until emulsified. Pour over the cauliflower and toss to combine.

Add half of the dry mix to the bowl and stir through then add the rest. Toss through and place cauliflower individually on a tray and bake for 30 minutes until crispy.

# Guacamole

*Vegan | Gluten free*
*Serves 4-6*

3 avocados, halved and stone removed
zest and juice of 1 lemon or lime
1 clove garlic, crushed
1 spring onion or 2 onion weed, finely sliced
1/4 cup roughly chopped fresh coriander
1/2 tsp salt
1/4 tsp cracked black pepper
sliced jalapeños (optional)

Scoop the flesh out of the avocados into a bowl and mash with a fork. Add the lemon or lime, garlic, spring onion, coriander, salt and pepper. Cut the third avocado into small dice (in the shell is easiest), then scoop into bowl and mix together. Top with jalapeños (if using).

# Rice 'n' Beans

*Vegan | Gluten free*
*Serves 6*

2 tablespoons extra-virgin olive oil or 1 tablespoon butter
1 red onion, finely chopped
1 red capsicum, cored, deseeded and diced or 1 stick celery, sliced
4 button mushrooms, diced
2 cloves garlic, crushed
1 chilli or smoked chipotle chilli, finely chopped (optional)
1 tablespoon cumin seeds, toasted then crushed or ground
1 tablespoon coriander seeds, toasted then crushed or ground
1 tsp caraway seeds, toasted then crushed or ground
1 cinnamon quill
1 cup long-grain white rice, rinsed or 1 cup long grain brown rice, rinsed
2 cups (500ml) water (for white rice)  or 700ml water (for brown rice)
400g can chopped tomatoes, passata or fresh tomatoes grated to remove skins
400g can black beans, drained and rinsed
1 tsp salt
1/4 tsp cracked black pepper
1 bay leaf
1/2 cup roughly chopped fresh coriander
juice of 1 lime

Preheat the oven to 160° C. Place an ovenproof dish in the oven while it's heating, or just the lid if you can use the base for frying. If you are using brown rice, cover well with hot water and leave to soak while you prepare the other ingredients.

Heat the olive oil in the base of the dish or a frying pan on a medium-high heat and add the onion, capsicum and mushrooms, fry for 1 minute then add the garlic, chilli (if using) and spices. Fry for another minute then add the rice (drain the water from the brown rice first, if using), fry for 1 minute.

Transfer to the warmed ovenproof dish (if using a frying pan) then add the water, tomatoes, black beans, salt, pepper and the bay leaf, cover and bake for 30 minutes for white rice or 50 minutes to 1 hour for brown rice. Check if cooked, then stir with a fork, remove from the oven and leave to steam for a while with the lid on.

Garnish with the coriander and a squeeze of lime juice.

# Pepitas

*Vegan | Gluten free*
*Makes 1 cup*

1 cup pumpkin seeds
1 tsp cumin seeds, toasted then crushed or ground
1 tsp ground cinnamon
1 tsp smoked sweet paprika
1 tsp extra-virgin olive oil
1 tsp maple syrup
1 tsp salt
1/4 tsp cracked black pepper

Preheat the oven to 160°C.

Measure all the ingredients into a roasting tray. Mix together to coat the seeds and bake for 10 minutes, stirring half way through cooking.

Cool and store in a jar – if there are any left!

# Veggie Burger

You can't beat a good burger, and the key is a tasty patty. These pea patties are scrumptious, succulent and can be made to suit the style of burger you are after. Don't scrimp on the oil for frying as plant-based proteins are pure protein with no fat marbling, I've added the coconut oil to compensate for this within the recipe. I love coleslaw with my burgers as it holds its juiciness for longer than lettuce. The summer and winter slaws (page 66 and 68) are perfect, along with a good smothering of your favourite chutney, relish, pesto, sauce or mayo to both the top and bottom of the burger buns. The classic accompaniment to a good burger is hot chips and the quick easy recipe (page 134) won't disappoint.

Flavouring herbs and spice combinations:
Chicken – thyme, rosemary, parsley, dried ground coriander.
Beef – black pepper, ground cumin, mustard, oregano, rosemary.
Pork – smoke paprika, smoke liquid, sage, marjoram.

As alternatives to the pea patty, either of the Tempeh Patty options (page 132) are awesome depending on whether you are going for an Asian style burger with wasabi mayo and Asian slaw or a Mediterranean style burger with a barbequed Portobello mushrooms (page 134) and melted blue cheese oozing over the patty. If you wanted to go for more of a Sloppy Joe style, add a dollop of the Mexican Mole Jackfruit (page 142) with some sliced avocado and pickled jalapenos.

## Vegan | Gluten free
## Makes 6 patties

1/2 cup psyllium husk mixed with ½ cup hot water
1/2 cup aquafaba
1 1/4 cup pea flour
1/4 cup brown rice flour
1 tablespoons coconut oil, refined, grated
2 tablespoon flavouring herbs and spices
1 tsp salt
2 tablespoons apple cider vinegar
2 tablespoons light soy sauce, tamari or coconut aminos
1/2 cup hot water
1/4 cup rice bran oil

Measure the psyllium and first quantity of hot water into a bowl, stir together roughly using a butter knife, leaving it lumpy. Add the aquafaba, pea flour, brown rice flour, coconut oil, flavourings, salt, apple cider vinegar, soy sauce and remaining water and stir together until it comes together as one mass. Shape into desired shape with wet hands and fry on a medium high heat until golden on each side, approximately 2 minutes with two tablespoons of oil at a time.

# Summer Curry with Onion Kulcha

*Utilising beautiful summer produce in this colourful curry makes it not only good looking but also really yummy. The paneer and onion kulcha are traditionally made with a leavened dough but for time-saving purposes I've deviated from that. Don't scrimp on the fat options or you won't get a good golden finish. If you are going to have sprouted lentils with the dish, you'll need to get them on a couple of days in advance.*

## Vegan | Gluten free
### Serves 4-6

### Curry
1/2 cup dried green lentils, soaked in water overnight
1 aubergine, cubed
1 tablespoon salt
1 tablespoon cumin seed
1 tablespoon coriander seeds
2 tablespoons fennel seeds
1 tsp cardamom seeds
1 tsp fenugreek seeds
1 tablespoon yellow mustard seeds
1/4 cup coconut oil or rice bran oil
1 onion, diced
1 orange capsicum, cored, deseeded and diced
1 tablespoon dried or fresh curry leaves (optional)
2 cloves garlic, sliced
1 tablespoon finely grated fresh turmeric , or ground
5 large tomatoes, grated into a bowl, skins discarded, or 400ml passata or canned
200ml water
2 tablespoons tamarind paste
2 cobs sweetcorn, kernels only
1 tsp salt
1/2 tsp cracked black pepper
1/2 cup roughly chopped fresh coriander or curry herb leaves

### Rice
1 cup brown basmati rice, rinsed
700ml water
1/2 tsp salt

### Onion Kulcha
2 cups flour (naan flour is ideal, but any wheat flour will do) or 1/2 cup each of buckwheat or chickpea, coconut flour, brown rice flour, tapioca flour
1/4 cup psyllium husk mixed with 1/2 cup hot water (gluten-free option only)
1/2 tsp salt
2 tablespoons melted ghee or coconut oil
3/4 cup milk, plant-based or dairy
300g paneer, or Dairy Ricotta (page 21), crumbled
4 tablespoons melted ghee or coconut oil

### To make the curry:
Two days before you want to make this dish, soak the lentils in water overnight. Next morning drain lentils through a sieve. Cover the sieve with a tea towel and rinse the lentils again at night, then again in the morning until they start to sprout. They are now ready to use.

Place the aubergine in a colander, sprinkle with salt and shake through. Leave to drain.

Prepare the vegetables and toast the spices (except the mustard seeds) in a dry pan until fragrant. Remove from the heat and grind into a powder.

Measure the mustard seeds into a pot on a high heat and dry toast until popping. Add the coconut oil, onion, capsicum and aubergine, and fry for 2 minutes. Add the curry leaves (if using) along with the garlic and cook for 30 seconds, then add the turmeric, spices, tomatoes, water and tamarind paste. Simmer for 15 minutes, until the aubergine starts to breakdown a little.

Lastly, add the sweetcorn and seasoning. Remove from the heat and top with the fresh coriander or curry herb leaves and the sprouted lentils.

Serve with steamed brown basmati rice, onion kulcha and your favourite pickle.

## To make the rice:

Place the rice, salt and water in a medium-sized pot. Put the lid on and bring to the boil, then turn down to simmer for 35 minutes. Stir with a fork, put the lid back on, turn off the heat and leave the rice to steam for 10 minutes.

## To make the Onion Kulcha:

Measure the flours, psyllium mix (if using gluten-free option) and salt into a bowl. Mix together with a butter knife, then add the oil and milk. Stir together until it forms one mass then tip the dough out on to a floured bench and knead until it has formed a smooth ball. Tip the bowl over it and leave it to rest.

Prepare the onion and cheese. Heat a hotplate, barbeque, cast-iron pan or griddle. Dust the bench and rolling pin with flour.

Cut the dough into eight pieces and shape each piece gently into rounds. Using your fingers, push each piece out to about 10cm. Place 1 teaspoon of cheese and a pinch of onion in the centre of each round. Pull in the edges all the way around, so it comes together with no gaps. Pinch together and push down gently to flatten a little. Roll the parcel gently and as flat as you can without the filling bursting out, about 15cm.

When the hotplate is smoking, put oil or ghee on and immediately add the kulcha, four at a time, if space allows. Cook for 1–2 minutes until they are bubbled and golden on top. Add another 2 tablespoons of fat to the pan and flip. Cook for another 1–2 minutes. Transfer to a tea towel on a cooling rack.

# Ragu with Potato au Gratin

When the colder weather arrives, we start to crave delicious warming comfort food. This recipe is a great one for those times when you just want to chuck the dinner in the oven and walk away from the kitchen for an hour while it cooks. Any type of beans or lentils could be used as an alternative to the plant protein, or plant-based sausages. The main tip I can give about cooking with plant-based proteins is they need fat and sauce. Plant-based proteins, including beans and lentils, are predominantly pure protein, which means you need to add fats separately. Braising is a great method of cookery for juicy, flavourful meals and perfect for fuss-free meals too.

## Vegan | Gluten free
## Serves 4-6

### Gratin

1 tablespoon butter, plant-based or dairy or extra-virgin olive oil
4 potatoes, scrubbed and thinly sliced (I use a Japanese mandolin)
1 shallot, thinly sliced
2 cloves garlic, thinly sliced
4 sprigs fresh thyme, leaves stripped
250g Gruyère cheese or plant-based mozzarella, grated
200ml cream, dairy or cashew
50ml water

### Ragu

3 tablespoons extra-virgin olive oil
2 shallots, halved
2 small red onions, halved
300g veggie meat or other plant protein
1 clove garlic, chopped
2 stalks celery, sliced
100g olives, pitted
1 stalk fresh rosemary, leaves stripped
400ml can chopped tomatoes or passata
200ml water
1/2 tsp salt
1/4 tsp cracked black pepper

To make the gratin, preheat the oven to 180°C.

Grease an ovenproof dish with the butter and alternately layer the potatoes, shallot, garlic, thyme and cheese, saving a little cheese for the top.

Mix the cream and water together and pour over the top evenly, sprinkle over the remaining cheese. Cover and bake at 180°C for 1 hour.

Test the potato is done by gently pushing a knife through the middle; it should easily go through the potato layers.

To make the ragu, heat an ovenproof dish in the oven (lid only if you can use the base on the stove top). Slowly heat the base of the dish or a heavy-based frying pan and add the olive oil, shallots and onions and fry for 2 minutes. Add the protein, garlic, celery, olives and rosemary. Sauté until beginning to colour.

Transfer to a warmed, ovenproof dish (if using a frying pan). Add the tomatoes, water, salt and pepper. Cover and bake at 180°C for 1 hour. Serve with your choice of steamed green vegetables.

# Roast Veggies with Crispy Chickpeas, Roasted Nuts and Tahini Mayo

*This one-tray, quick and easy recipe is nutritious and delicious, a perfect family-friendly dinner.*

Vegan | Gluten free
Serves 4-6

2 tablespoons rice bran or any neutral oil
4 potatoes, scrubbed clean and chopped into bite-sized pieces
4 carrots, scrubbed clean and chopped into bite-sized pieces
2 kumara, scrubbed clean and chopped into bite-sized pieces
2 beetroots, scrubbed clean and chopped into bite-sized pieces
2 parsnips, scrubbed clean and chopped into bite-sized pieces
2 tablespoons extra-virgin olive oil
3 tablespoons roughly chopped fresh rosemary
1 tsp salt
1/4 tsp cracked black pepper
1 broccoli, cut into small florets
1 cauliflower, cut into small florets
2 tablespoons extra-virgin olive oil (extra)
400g can or home-cooked chickpeas
1 cup raw mixed nuts
1 tsp smoked sweet paprika or ground cumin
1/2 tsp salt
1/4 tsp cracked black pepper
2 tablespoons olive or neutral oil
1/2 cup roughly chopped parsley or coriander
1/2 cup olives, sliced (optional)

## Tahini Mayo (Makes 1 cup)

1/4 cup tahini
1/4 cup plain yoghurt, dairy or alternative
1 clove garlic, crushed
zest and juice of 2 lemons
2 tsp pomegranate molasses (optional)
1/4 cup extra-virgin olive oil
1/4 tsp salt
a few grinds of black pepper

Preheat the oven to 200°C. Measure the rice bran oil into a large roasting pan and put into the oven while it is heating.

Meanwhile, put the root vegetables in a large bowl and toss together with the olive oil, rosemary, salt and cracked black pepper. Remove the hot pan from the oven and carefully transfer the seasoned vegetables and roast for 45 minutes to 1 hour, turning a couple of times during cooking.

Add the broccoli and cauliflower to the seasoning bowl with the additional 2 tablespoons olive oil and toss to coat. (These will be added towards the end of cooking.)

Drain the chickpeas, rinse and pour onto a dry tea towel or paper towel to remove moisture, then make the Tahini Mayo.

After 30 minutes or so, add the broccoli and cauliflower to the roasting pan and cook for a further 10 minutes. Add the chickpeas, mixed nuts, smoked sweet paprika, salt, black pepper and olive oil to the bowl and toss to coat. Pour into another roasting pan or ovenproof dish and place in the oven. Cook for 10 minutes, giving it a mix after 5 minutes.

To finish the dish, remove the roasting pans from the oven and tip the chickpea and nut mix on top of the other roasted vegetables. Scatter over the parsley and olives and drizzle liberally with the Tahini Mayo.

To make the Tahini Mayo, place the tahini, plain yoghurt, garlic, lemons, pomegranate molasses, extra-virgin olive oil, salt and pepper in a food processor or bowl and whizz or mix together well until smooth.

Store in a covered jar in the fridge (it will thicken when refrigerated).

# Ratatouille

*This is the perfect 'eat a rainbow' everyday dish. It's also a lovely Christmas dinner option or to take along to a celebration meal. You could use either of the plant protein options in this book instead of beans or a store-brought veggie mince. Choose vegetables that are a similar size, so they fit into each other more easily.*

## Vegan | Gluten free
## Serves 6-8

1/4 cup extra-virgin olive oil
1 red onion, diced
1 stick celery, diced
2 cloves garlic, sliced
2 tablespoons balsamic vinegar
a pinch of sugar
700g tomatoes, skins removed (grated, passata or canned)
200ml water
2 sprigs rosemary, leaves removed and roughly chopped
1 tablespoon roughly chopped fresh or dried oregano
1/4 cup olives, pitted
400g can butter, pinto or kidney beans, drained and rinsed
3 sprigs fresh basil, roughly chopped
1 tsp salt
1/4 tsp cracked black pepper
1 aubergine, cut into 3mm slices (if it's a large aubergine, cut in half lengthways first)
1 red capsicum, deseeded and chopped into three pieces lengthways before slicing
1 orange capsicum, deseeded and chopped into three pieces lengthways before slicing
1 zucchini, cut into 3mm slices
1 potato or kumara, cut into 3mm slices
2 tablespoons extra-virgin olive oil

Heat the olive oil in a large pan on a medium-high heat. Add the onion, celery and garlic and fry for 3 minutes. Stir in the balsamic vinegar, sugar, tomatoes, water, half the rosemary, oregano, olives and beans and simmer gently for 20 minutes.

Preheat the oven to 180°C. When the sauce in the pan has thickened, about 30 minutes, remove from the heat and add the basil and seasonings and stir through. Pour into an ovenproof dish drizzled with olive oil.

Starting from the outside, arrange the sliced vegetables on top, so they stand upright but lean against each other. Drizzle with the second measure of olive oil and sprinkle with the remaining rosemary. Cover and bake for 11/2 hours.

Remove from the oven and serve with fresh bread or a leafy salad.

# Stuffing Stuffed Vegetables, Hasselback Potatoes, Ale and Miso Gravy, Yorkies and Garlic Butter Greens

*We have a Yorkshireman in the house and he loves a traditional roast dinner. This stuffing is the ultimate protein-rich mash up of tempeh, tofu and a nut roast along with a delicious herby stuffing. Use seasonal vegetables; if capsicums aren't available use a small pumpkin cut in half and seeds scooped out (artichokes or aubergine could also be used). The easy way to prepare hasselback potatoes is to place a wooden spoon alongside each potato to ensure you don't cut too far through it.*

## Stuffing Stuffed Vegetables

*Vegan | Gluten free*
*Serves 4*

1 slice bread, wheat or gluten free, torn into small pieces
2 cloves garlic, crushed
1 red onion, finely diced
2 tablespoons extra-virgin olive oil
1 tsp sesame oil
1 egg (or 2 tablespoons chia or ground flaxseed soaked in 1/3 cup water for 10 minutes)
1/2 cup roughly chopped fresh herbs (e.g. thyme, sage, parsley, mint)
zest and juice of 1 lemon
300g tempeh, grated
300g tofu including the water, crumbled or mashed
1 cup mixed nuts, roughly chopped in the food processor
1 tsp salt
1/4 tsp cracked black pepper
4 capsicums, top removed to remove seeds but retain stalk so it can go back on for cooking
4 field mushrooms or large tomatoes, tops removed to remove seeds and save for cooking or 1 marrow or kamo kamo, sliced into thick rounds and seeds removed
4–6 floury potatoes or kumara, scrubbed and sliced halfway through at 3mm intervals
1 head garlic, halved width ways
2 tablespoons extra-virgin olive oil

Preheat the oven to 180°C. Stir together the bread, garlic, onion, olive oil, sesame oil, egg, herbs, lemon, tempeh, tofu, nuts, salt and pepper.

Oil a roasting tray. Stuff the capsicums, mushrooms, marrow pieces or tomatoes with the stuffing. Pop the tops back on the capsicums and tomatoes and arrange in the roasting tray with the prepared potatoes and garlic. Drizzle with the olive oil and season.

Bake for 1 hour until the capsicums are cooked and starting to slump.

# Mushroom, Ale and Miso Gravy

An essential part of any roast dinner, this gravy is packed with umami flavours and is so delicious. Make sure you don't boil it after adding the miso as it will kill off the probiotic goodies.

*Vegan | Gluten free*
*Serves 4*

2 tablespoons extra-virgin olive oil
1 tablespoon butter, plant-based or dairy
1 leek or 1 onion, halved and sliced
1 stick celery, sliced
4 Swiss brown mushrooms, sliced
2 cloves garlic, sliced
300ml ale or stout
800ml water + 1 tsp vegetable bouillon powder (or use liquid vegetable stock)
2 bay leaves
2 pieces of seaweed, wakame or kelp (optional)
6 sprigs of thyme, leaves removed
3 sprigs sage, roughly chopped or 1 tablespoon dried
2 tablespoons cornflour or tapioca flour
1/4 cup water
2 tablespoons miso paste
1 tablespoon light soy sauce, tamari or coconut aminos
1 sprig parsley, finely chopped
1/4 tsp black pepper

Heat the olive oil and butter in a medium pot. When the butter has melted add the leek, celery and mushrooms and sauté, stirring occasionally, until they start to colour.

Add the garlic, stir through, then deglaze the pan with the beer and simmer for 1 minute. Add the liquid stock, bay leaves, seaweed, thyme and sage. Bring to the boil, then turn down to a low simmer and cook for 20–30 minutes.

In a small bowl, mix the cornflour with the water. Scoop a ladleful of the gravy into another small bowl, mix in the miso paste and stir until smooth. Add the cornflour mix to the gravy, stirring well, and bring to a simmer. Stir in the miso mix and add the soy sauce, parsley and pepper. Remove from the heat and pour into a gravy boat to serve.

# Garlic Butter Greens

This recipe is very versatile and you can use any greens available. Some of our favourites are silverbeet, kale, broccoli, peas, green beans, nasturtium greens, dandelion greens, onion weed, ruruhau (wild mustard greens) – the options are endless, really. You can use the roast garlic from the stuffing stuffed vegetables for this dish which adds a lovely depth of flavour.

*Vegan | Gluten free*
*Serves 4*

1–2 tablespoons butter, plant-based or dairy
4 cloves garlic, crushed or roasted and puréed
8 cups roughly chopped leafy greens
1/2 tsp salt
1/4 tsp black pepper

Melt the butter in a pan on a medium heat and add the garlic. Gently sauté for 2 minutes.

Add the greens with a dash of water, salt and pepper. Cover with a lid and turn the heat to high. Turn the greens over every now and then to ensure even cooking until wilted, about 2minutes.

Remove from the heat and serve with a sprinkling of hemp parmesan, if desired.

# Yorkies

*These are so lovely and light, like little soufflés with hollow centres to hold the gravy, and are an integral part of the meal according to my family. The most important part of making Yorkshire puddings is to ensure the oil is super hot before you pour the batter in it. I use a muffin tin to make my Yorkies but any high-heat, ovenproof tin can be used; you can even make one big one in a roasting tin. In fact, this is how you make 'toad in the hole' by adding fried sausages and onions to the tray along with the yorkie batter.*

## Vegan | Gluten free
## Makes 15

1 cup flour, plain or gluten-free mix, sifted
1/2 tsp salt
1/4 tsp pepper
200ml milk, unsweetened plant-based or dairy
4 eggs
85ml rice bran or preferred neutral flavoured oil

## Vegan and gluten-free option

1/2 cup chickpea flour
1/2 cup cornflour
1/2 tsp salt
1/4 tsp pepper
100ml aquafaba
1 tsp cream of tartar
2 heaped tsp baking powder
220ml unsweetened plant milk

Add the flour and seasoning into a large jug or bowl. Make a well in the center and whisk the milk and eggs in to make a smooth batter, chill for 20 minutes. Measure one tablespoon of oil into each space in your muffin tin, then place in the oven and preheat to 200°C. Remove the heated tin from the oven and pour about two tablespoons of batter into each section as quickly as possible and put back in the oven. Cook for 15 minutes or so until golden brown and puffed up. Remove the Yorkshire puddings from the tin and serve immediately.

# Penne 'n' Cheese

My version of Mac 'n' Cheese: the ultimate comfort food. I love wholemeal dried pasta, it contains more fibre than regular pasta and tastes great. With added veggies for flavour and colour, this doesn't have to be an unhealthy meal.

## Vegan | Gluten free
## Serves 4-6

200g butter, plant-based or dairy or rice bran oil
1 onion, finely diced
1 carrot, finely diced
150g plant-based bacon or hotdog, diced (optional)
1 clove garlic, crushed
3/4 cup flour
1 litre milk, plant-based or dairy (rice milk is good for a neutral flavour)
1 tsp vegetable stock powder
1 tsp mustard powder
1 tablespoon dried oregano
1 tsp fresh thyme leaves
3 cup (300g) grated cheese, plant-based or dairy
1 tsp salt
1/2 tsp cracked black pepper
2 tablespoons salt (for cooking pasta)
400g wholemeal penne pasta or gluten-free penne pasta
6 Brussels sprouts, halved
1/4 cauliflower, cut into bite-sized pieces
1/4 broccoli, cut into bite-sized pieces
50g cheese, tasty or vegan, grated
1 tomato or tamarillo (peeled), sliced
finely grated parmesan, dairy or vegan

## Gluten free option
Replace flour with:
1/3 cup cornflour + 1/2 cup water

Grease an ovenproof dish. Put a big pot of water on to boil with the lid on. Melt the butter or heat the oil in a pan, then add the onion, carrot, bacon and garlic. Fry for 1 minute. Add the flour and stir while cooking for 1 minute on a medium-high heat.

Gradually add the milk, one cupful at a time, stirring constantly to avoid lumps. After the second addition of milk, add the vegetable stock powder, mustard powder and herbs.

When all the milk has been incorporated, add the grated cheese and stir through to melt. Season with salt and pepper.

If not using immediately, push a piece of baking paper down onto the top to prevent a skin forming.

## To make the gluten-free version:

After frying the onion, carrot, bacon and garlic, add the milk to the pan along with the vegetable stock powder, mustard powder and herbs. Simmer for 10 minutes.

Meanwhile, mix the cornflour with the water until smooth, then add to the sauce. Stir well until thickened. Add the cheese and mix until smooth.

Preheat the oven to 180°C. Add the salt to the pot of boiling water, then add the pasta. Stir and cook until al dente.

Add the Brussels sprouts, cauliflower and broccoli and cook for a further 30 seconds. Drain through a colander then stir into the prepared sauce.

Spoon into the greased ovenproof dish and top with the second measure of cheese. Arrange the sliced tomato or tamarillo on top.

Bake for 15 minutes until bubbling and golden. Top with finely grated parmesan, dairy or vegan, and serve.

# Spaghetti Bolognese with Chargrilled Broccoli

*Spaghetti Bolognese is a firm family favourite. This recipe uses vegetable protein-based mince. My favourite is Quorn brand. Alternatively, you can use brown lentils, cooked or canned, or rehydrated TVP, or use the Cottage Pie mince from page 140.*

*Vegan | Gluten free*
*Serves 4*

2 tablespoons butter, plant-based or dairy
1 onion, finely diced
3 mushrooms, finely diced or grated
1 carrot, 1 stick of celery or 1 capsicum, finely diced
2 cloves garlic, crushed
300g plant-based mince or alternative
1/3 cup red wine or 2 tablespoons Balsamic Reduction (page 39)
700ml jar passata or 2 x 400g cans chopped tomatoes
400ml water
1 tsp thyme leaves
2 tsp sage leaves, roughly chopped
2 tsp oregano leaves, roughly chopped
2 tsp rosemary leaves, roughly chopped
2 bay leaves
3 tablespoons pine nuts (optional)
1/2 tsp salt
1/4 tsp cracked black pepper
2 tablespoons salt
400g dried spaghetti, wholemeal or gluten-free
1/2 cup hemp parmesan or Parmesan cheese, grated

Heat the olive oil and butter in a pan on high heat. When the butter has melted, add the onion, mushrooms and carrot. Sauté for 2 minutes, then add the garlic and mince. Sauté for another 2 minutes, then add the red wine, stir through and simmer for 30 seconds. Add the passata, water, herbs and pine nuts (if using) and simmer for 25 minutes, stirring occasionally. When thickened, season with salt and pepper.

Meanwhile, three-quarter fill a pot with water, cover and bring to the boil. Add the second measure of salt and pasta, stir and cook for 10 minutes or until just cooked through, al dente. Remove from the heat and drain pasta in a colander, add to the sauce and mix through gently, using tongs. Add 1/4 cup of parmesan to the pasta and use the rest to sprinkle on top, as desired. Serve with Chargrilled Broccoli.

# Chargrilled Broccoli

1 head broccoli
3 tablespoons extra-virgin olive oil
2 sprigs fresh oregano, leaves roughly chopped
1 small sprig of fresh rosemary, stripped and leaves roughly chopped
zest and juice of 1 lemon
1/2 tsp salt
1/4 tsp pepper
1 tablespoon water
1/3 cup hemp parmesan (page 22)
2–3 sprigs of fresh basil, torn into pieces

Preheat a chargrill pan, a grill or a cast-iron frying pan until smoking hot. Cut the broccoli into quarters lengthways and place in a bowl. Drizzle the olive oil over the top, sprinkle with the herbs, lemon, salt and pepper. Mix to coat the broccoli pieces.

Press each piece of broccoli firmly onto the grill and cook, without moving, for 1–2 minutes, until well coloured. Turn and press down again with the back of a spatula to sear. Cook for another 1–2 minutes, then add water and cover with a lid and steam for 30 seconds. Remove the lid, check the broccoli is cooked all the way through by inserting a knife through the thickest part, it should go through easily.

Serve alongside the Spaghetti Bolognese with a squeeze of lemon and a sprinkling of hemp parmesan and basil.

# Kumara, Cashew and Cauliflower Curry

*This kumara and cashew curry is nutty, creamy and a real crowd-pleaser. It is perfect for mild curry lovers as spice doesn't need to be hot to be full of delicious flavours. Kashmiri rice is a delicious, nutritious, earthy-brown rice dish with raisins, coconut and a hint of saffron.*

## Vegan | Gluten-Free

### Serves 6

2 cups raw cashew nuts
300ml hot water
1 tsp cumin seeds
1/2 tsp fenugreek seeds
1 tsp cardamom seeds
1 tablespoon fennel seeds
1 tablespoon coriander seeds
1 tablespoon yellow mustard seeds
2 tablespoons coconut oil, virgin or refined or ghee
8 curry leaves, fresh or dried (optional)
1 onion, finely chopped
1 fresh chilli, sliced (optional)
3 clove garlic, finely chopped
1 red kumara, scrubbed and diced
400g can chopped tomatoes, then fill the can with 400ml water
400ml can coconut cream, then fill the can with 400ml water
1 tablespoon finely grated fresh ginger
1 cinnamon quill
1 tablespoon ground turmeric
1/4 cauliflower, cut into small florets
1 tablespoon coconut vinegar or rice vinegar
1 tablespoon light soy sauce, tamari or coconut aminos
1/4 cup ground almonds
1 tsp cracked black pepper and salt

## Kashmiri Rice

1 cup brown basmati rice
2 tablespoons raisins
1 pinch saffron (optional)
1/2 tsp salt
750ml water
4 tablespoons coconut chips or thread
1 tablespoon ghee or butter, plant-based or dairy (optional)

Measure the cashew nuts and hot water into a jug and leave to soften for one hour.

Place the cumin, fenugreek, cardamom, fennel and coriander seeds in a dry pan and toast over a high heat, shaking the pan often, until they start to release their scent. Remove from the heat and cool a little, then grind to a powder in a spice grinder or mortar and pestle.

Measure the mustard seeds into a large pot on a high heat, cook until just starting to pop. Immediately add the coconut oil, curry leaves (if using), onion, chilli (if using), garlic, kumara and ground spices. Sauté for 1 minute, then add the soaked cashew nuts along with the soaking water, chopped tomatoes, coconut cream, water, ginger, cinnamon quill and turmeric. Bring to the boil then turn down to a gentle simmer for 45 minutes, stirring a couple of times during cooking.

Add the cauliflower, vinegar, soy sauce, almonds and seasoning, stir through and simmer for another 10 minutes. Serve with the Kashmiri Rice.

## To make the Kasmiri Rice:

Rinse the rice well and tip into a pot. Add the raisins, saffron (if using), salt, water and coconut. Cover with the lid and bring to the boil. Turn it down to a simmer immediately and stir with a fork. Replace the lid and simmer until you can't see any water, about 25 minutes.

Gently stir and add the ghee. Replace the lid and remove from the heat to steam for 10 minutes. Give it a final, gentle stir with a fork while it sits. Serve with the curry and your favourite chutney or pickle.

To make a simple raita combine 1 small clove garlic, 1 cup fresh mint leaves, 1/2 tsp salt, 1 cup plain thick yoghurt, zest and juice of 1 lemon and pepper into a blender and whizz till smooth. Stir through 1/4 cucumber, grated and drained.

# Lasagne

*I tested this recipe a good few times and, for the kids' benefit, I have settled on this version. Yes, there are a lot of steps, so that you can make the whole dish from scratch, but you absolutely don't have to. Shop-bought lasagne sheets are available in gluten-free or regular. I find the art of disguise is key for happy mealtimes all round. If you have zucchini lovers in your home, add some chargrilled or sautéed zucchini, but if you want to hide it use the grated option. Gluten flour is the concentrated protein from the wheat flour and brings a greater elasticity to the dough.*

*Note: Excess pasta sheets can be hand cut into pappardelle (thick 1.5cm wide strips) or fettuccini. Cook in salted, boiling water until al dente. Mix through some pesto and add fresh tomatoes, olives, artichoke hearts and hemp parmesan.*

## Vegan | Gluten free
### Serves 8 (Makes 21 x 28cm dish)

### Pasta

3 eggs
2 cups wholemeal flour
2 tablespoons gluten flour (optional)
1 tablespoon extra-virgin olive oil
1 tablespoon water

### Gluten-free Pasta

1 1/2 cup chickpea flour
1/2 cup tapioca flour
1 tablespoon extra-virgin olive oil
1/4 cup ground flaxseed mixed with 1/4 cup water, stir and leave to absorb for 5 minutes
1/4 cup psyllium husk mixed with 3/4 cup hottest tap water, mix together until it forms one mass
2 tablespoons water

### Bolognese Sauce

See recipe on page 162

### Smoked Aubergine Sauce

1 aubergine, smoked, peeled and roughly chopped
200g butter or neutral oil
1 clove garlic, sliced
3/4 cup flour or 1/3 cup cornflour mixed with 1/2 cup water
1 litre milk, rice or dairy
1 tsp vegetable stock powder
1 tsp mustard powder
1 tablespoon dried oregano
3 cups grated cheese, plant-based or dairy
a pinch of salt and pepper

### Chargrilled Zucchini

2 zucchini, grated (then squeezed in a tea towel to remove excess moisture) or cut into 0.5cm slices on the diagonal
1 tablespoon extra-virgin olive oil
1 sprig rosemary, leaves stripped and finely chopped
a pinch of salt and black pepper

### To Finish

2–3 tomatoes, sliced
a few shakes of salt
a few grinds of pepper

## To make the Pasta:

Measure the flour, eggs and olive oil to the food processor and whizz till it comes together in one mass, using one tablespoon at a time of water if it's a little dry. Or stir together with a butter knife. Tip out onto the bench and knead to form a smooth ball. Cover with a bowl and leave to rest for 10 minutes. Cut the ball into four pieces and roll out one piece at a time as flat as you can by hand or using a pasta machine. Dust with flour to prevent sticking. If using a machine go to mark 5 for regular flour or to mark four for gluten-free. If rolling by hand, roll into long rectangles about 1mm thick. Using the ovenproof dish as a measure, cut the sheets into appropriate sized pieces with a pizza cutter if you have one.

## To make the Gluten-free Pasta:

Measure the chickpea and tapioca flour into a bowl with the olive oil. Add the flaxseed and psyllium mixtures and mix well using a butter knife. Mix until it comes together in one mass, adding the water 1 tablespoon at a time if needed.

Dust the bench with tapioca flour, then tip the dough out of the bowl and knead to form a smooth ball. Cut into four equal pieces. Working with one piece at a time (leave the rest under a bowl or tea towel) and dusting with flour when needed, use a rolling pin to roll each piece into a rectangular shape.

Then roll through the widest roller on your pasta machine, mark 1. Follow on by rolling it through each of the 4 thickness settings one by one, dusting the dough with plenty of tapioca flour if sticky.

## To make the Smoked Aubergine Sauce:

Put the whole aubergine straight onto the gas flame or under a flame grill, leave to become blackened and charred before turning. When the whole thing is collapsing and smoking, remove it from the heat, place in a bowl and cover. When it is cool enough to touch, peel away the blackened skin.

Melt the butter or heat the oil in a pan, then add the garlic and aubergine. Fry for 1 minute. Add the flour and stir while cooking for 1 minute on a medium-high heat. Gradually add the milk, one cupful at a time, stirring constantly to avoid lumps. After the second addition of

milk, add the vegetable stock powder, mustard powder and oregano. When all the milk has been incorporated, add the grated cheese and stir through to melt. Season with salt and pepper. If not using immediately, push a piece of baking paper down onto the top to prevent a skin forming.

To make the gluten-free version, omit the flour. Add the milk to the fried aubergine and garlic and bring almost to the boil, adding the vegetable stock, mustard powder and oregano. Mix the cornflour with half a cup of water, then add to the sauce, stirring well until thickened. Add the cheese and mix until smooth and season with salt and pepper.

## To make the Chargrilled Zucchini:

Place the zucchini, olive oil and rosemary into a bowl and toss together. Make sure the grill is smoking hot. Place one piece of zucchini on the grill at a time and push it down, leaving enough room around each piece so you can easily flip it. Leave them for 1 minute or so before checking. When it is a dark, golden colour or has char lines, flip over and press down again with the back of the spatula. Cook for another minute or until lines appear. Remove from the grill and set aside. Repeat until all zucchini has been cooked. Season with salt and pepper.

## To assemble the Lasagne:

When all the elements are ready preheat the oven to 180°C. Grease the ovenproof dish with olive oil and spoon in a layer of Bolognese sauce. Cover with a single layer of pasta. Top this with one-third of the aubergine sauce and half of the grated zucchini. Arrange a single layer of pasta sheets over this, then another layer of the Bolognese sauce, another layer of pasta with the second third of the aubergine sauce and the other half of the grated zucchini. Then a layer of pasta and the remaining Bolognese sauce. Arrange the final layer of pasta and the remaining aubergine sauce. Place tomato slices on top and sprinkle with salt and pepper. Bake for 1 hour until bubbling at the sides and golden. Serve with a big leafy green salad.

# Five-spice Fried Rice

*A quick stir-fry is a must for busy families. Always stir-fry on the highest heat and keep the ingredients moving in the pan or wok. Freezing the tofu creates a different texture with crispy bits, but it's not essential – you can just use firm tofu and omit the squeezing! Remember to take tofu from the freezer in the morning for your evening meal. I always keep my fresh ginger in a sealed container in the freezer and grate as needed with a fine microplane grater. I find this is the easiest way to add ginger to dishes and drinks with the minimum amount of effort and mess.*

**Vegan | Gluten free**
**Serves 4-6**

1 1/2 cups white jasmine rice, rinsed well
3 cups (740ml) water
2 cloves garlic, crushed
1 tablespoon frozen ginger, grated with a microplane
1/2 cup light soy sauce, tamari or coconut aminos
1 tsp toasted sesame oil
300g tofu, frozen then defrosted and squeezed to remove excess water
1/2 cup coconut or rice bran oil
200g fresh pineapple, cored and chopped into chunks
1 onion or leek, thinly sliced
1 carrot, thinly sliced
2 sticks celery, thinly sliced
4 button mushrooms, thinly sliced
1 tablespoon five-spice powder
1/2 broccoli, cut into small florets
1/2 cauliflower, cut into small florets
1/4 red cabbage, very finely sliced
2 tablespoons Chinese cooking wine or mirin (optional)

Measure the rice and water into a pot, cover and bring to the boil, then reduce to a simmer. Give it a quick stir with a fork, replace the lid and cook for 15 minutes. Give it another gentle stir with a fork and remove from the heat. Keep the lid on and steam for 10 minutes. Tip the rice out into a large bowl to cool.

Measure the garlic, ginger, soy sauce and sesame oil into a container. Crumble the tofu in uneven pieces into the marinade and set aside.

Drain the marinade off the tofu through a sieve, give it a gentle squeeze to remove as much moisture as you can and put the marinade aside for later. Melt the coconut oil in a wok or similar on a high heat. Add the tofu and stir-fry, moving it often to prevent burning. When the tofu is crisp, take it out of the wok using a slotted spoon and set aside.

Using the oil that's left in your wok, stir-fry the pineapple, leaving it to colour before flipping over. Add the onion, carrot, celery, mushrooms and the five-spice powder. Stir-fry for 2 minutes, then add the broccoli, cauliflower, red cabbage, cooking wine (if using) and left over marinade. Stir-fry for another minute. Lastly, add the rice and the crispy tofu, and mix through so the rice is touching the wok in places (to get some crispy rice). Cook for another minute. Remove from the heat and serve.

# Gnocchi with Sunshine Sauce and Pistachios

Gnocchi are little dumplings, a form of pasta, made with potatoes. Traditionally egg and flour is added to form a soft dough. Baking the potato first ensures the mash is dry, which helps keep the mixture light instead of stodgy. I find that 'dirty' potatoes (i.e. not pre-washed) roast more satisfactorily giving you a fluffier drier mash. When we have baked potatoes for dinner, I always make extra so that I can make gnocchi the next day. Always scoop the potato out of the skin and mash while it's still warm, as the starches in the potato change once cold. If you want to make the kumara or pumpkin versions it is important to use the 'drier' varieties. I find the red kumara are best for this and the buttercup pumpkins are definitely the ones to use. Any flour will work in this recipe: plain, wholemeal or gluten-free premixed flour. Cook the potatoes at the same time as the Sunshine Sauce veggies and you can totally use red capsicums and tomatoes for this sauce.

## Vegan | Gluten free
## Serves 4

1kg potatoes, red/purple kumara or buttercup pumpkin
1 cup flour, plain, wholemeal or gluten-free premixed flour
1 clove garlic, crushed
1 tsp salt
1/2 tsp pepper
1 egg (or 1 tablespoon ground flaxseed mixed with 2 tablespoons of water)

### Sunshine Sauce

2 yellow capsicums, cored and deseeded
6 yellow tomatoes, cored and halved
1 red onion, sliced
2 cloves garlic
2 tablespoons extra-virgin olive oil
1 tsp salt
1/4 tsp black pepper
3 sprigs basil
400g can cannellini or butter beans, drained

### To Serve

1/4 cup grated Parmesan or hemp parmesan (page 22)
3 tablespoons shelled pistachio nuts
fresh basil leaves

Preheat the oven to 190°C. Prick the potatoes with a fork then bake until a knife goes through easily, about 45–60 minutes.

To make the Sunshine Sauce, place the veggies and garlic in a roasting tray and drizzle the olive oil over the top, season and bake for 15 minutes. Remove from the oven. Cool then blend with the basil in a blender or food processor until smooth. Push the mixture through a sieve, discard the roughage. Pour into a pot and add the beans. Simmer for 10 minutes. Check seasoning and set aside.

When the potatoes are cooked, remove from the oven and set aside until cool enough to handle. Cut in half, scoop out the potato flesh into a large bowl and mash well (eat the skins with some butter, salt and pepper). Add the flour, garlic, salt, pepper and egg to the bowl and, using a butter knife, mix together until a dough forms. Tip out on to a floured surface and knead lightly to form a ball. Cut into quarters and roll each piece into a long sausage. Cut each roll into approximately 1/2 cm pieces. Keep sufficiently floured to stop sticking.

Put a large pan of water on to boil. When boiling, add 1 tablespoon of salt and carefully place about one-third of the gnocchi in the water. Give the pan a jiggle so they don't stick. When they float, they are ready. Remove with a slotted spoon into a colander, drizzle with olive oil and shake gently to coat. Repeat until all the gnocchi are cooked.

To serve you can either simply pour the sauce over the gnocchi and top with Parmesan, pistachios and basil leaves. Or pour the sauce over, top with parmesan and a drizzle of olive oil and bake for 10 minutes. Alternatively, fry the gnocchi in batches in olive oil and a knob of butter until golden and crispy before adding the sauce and garnishes.

# Pad Thai

*A traditional stir fried noodle dish which everyone loves, with a couple of optional additions and alternatives to cater for dietary requirements and add a little texture to this Thai classic. Serve the noodles topped with the tofu, peanuts, shallots, cucumber, a squeeze of fresh lime juice and crispy fried eggs.*

## Vegan | Gluten free
### Serves 6

200g thin rice noodles
1/4 cup rice bran oil
1 tsp toasted sesame oil
2 shallots, finely sliced
300g firm tofu, sliced in half lengthways, then again width-ways to make thin squares or mashed or 2 eggs, whisked
1 orange capsicum, cored deseeded and sliced
1 clove garlic, sliced
2 tablespoons finely grated ginger
1 zucchini, sliced on the diagonal
1 cob sweetcorn, kernels removed
1 bok choy, white part sliced into 5mm pieces width-ways and leaves roughly chopped lengthways
1/4 cup light soy sauce, tamari or coconut aminos
2 tablespoons mirin
1 tablespoon sweet soy sauce (optional)
1/2 cucumber, half lengthways then diagonal slices
1/2 cup Sichuan Peanuts, crushed
1 lime, cut into wedges

### Sichuan Peanuts

2 cups peanuts
1 tablespoon Sichuan pepper, crushed
1 tsp peanut or rice bran oil
1/2 tsp salt

### Fried Eggs

1/4 cup rice bran oil
6 eggs

Place the noodles in a heatproof bowl or pot and pour boiling water over the top to completely submerge the noodles. Move the noodles around with a fork, then leave to soak for 10 minutes. When they are soft, drain and cover with cold water.

Heat the rice bran and sesame oils in a wok or large frying pan on a medium-high heat. Add the shallots and fry, moving them around often, until they are golden brown and crisp. Remove with a slotted spoon to a wooden bowl or a bowl lined with a paper towel.

Add the tofu slices to the hot oil. Cook until coloured before turning to cook on the other side. When both sides are crispy and nicely coloured, remove from the oil with a slotted spoon to a separate bowl and sprinkle with soy sauce.

Add the capsicum, garlic and ginger to the pan and stir-fry for 1 minute before adding zucchini, corn and white parts of the bok choy. Fry for 1 minute. If adding eggs or mashed tofu do so now. Fry for 2 minutes then add the drained noodles and green tops of the bok choy, along with the soy sauce, mirin and sweet soy (if using). Stir-fry for a further 2 minutes.

To make the Fried Eggs, fry one at a time using a spoon to baste them with the oil, so they are crispy at the sides and opaque on the tops. Remove from the heat. Repeat for all.

To make the Sichuan Peanuts, preheat the oven to 180°C. Add the peanuts, Sichuan pepper, oil and salt to a roasting dish. Bake for 15–20 minutes, agitate the dish a couple of times for even cooking. Remove from the oven and allow to cool. (Store in a jar.)

Serve the noodles topped with the pre-cooked tofu, peanuts, shallots, cucumber, a squeeze of fresh lime juice and the fried eggs.

# Mushroom Stroganoff with Kasha

*The ultimate comfort food, this rich creamy dish from Russia is totally delicious. My version has big chunks of mushrooms instead of the original beef, and red kidney beans for protein. Served with earthy kasha which is toasted buckwheat groats which are a staple in Eastern Europe and absolutely delicious if cooked well. They can get mushy if cooked for too long, so I like to leave them to steam as you would when cooking rice. The addition of a little knob of butter helps the groats not to stick together. You could substitute for short-grain brown rice if you want to.*

## Vegan | Gluten free
## Serves 4

60g butter, plant or dairy
1 tablespoon extra-virgin olive oil or neutral oil
1 onion, diced
1 tsp caraway seeds, dry toasted and ground (you could leave whole)
2 sticks celery, sliced
1 capsicum, cut into large dice
200g Swiss button mushrooms, halved
4 large portobello mushrooms, quartered
3 cloves garlic, crushed
1/4 cup Riesling or other white wine (optional)
2 tablespoons tomato paste
400 can or cooked kidney beans, drained
500ml cream, cashew or dairy
200ml water
2 tsp vegetable stock powder
1 tablespoon mustard powder
2 bay leaves
1 tsp salt
1/2 tsp black pepper
1 cup buckwheat groats or kasha
1 3/4 cups water
1 tsp salt
1 tablespoon butter, plant-based or dairy
1/2 cup finely chopped parsley
1 tsp salt
1/2 tsp black pepper
1 lemon, halved

Heat the butter and olive oil in a pot on a medium heat until butter has melted. Add the onions, caraway seeds, celery, capsicum and mushrooms. Sauté for 5 minutes. Add the garlic, cook for a further minute, then add the wine (if using). Stir through and add the tomato paste, kidney beans, cream, water, stock powder, mustard powder and bay leaves. Simmer for 20 minutes.

Meanwhile, cook the kasha. Toast the buckwheat groats in a dry pan, shaking constantly for a couple of minutes, then add the water and salt. Cover and bring to the boil, turn down to a gentle simmer and cook for 15 minutes. Stir with a fork, add the butter, then remove from the heat. Leave to steam for 5 minutes with the lid on. Stir the parsley through the kasha. Season the stroganoff and serve with a squeeze of lemon.

# Baked Beans with Polenta and Avocado Salsa

*The key to baked beans is baking them. I know it sounds ridiculous, but unless you bake them they will break down more like refried beans, but we want baked beans, like from the can... but better! Aduki beans are super versatile and cook faster than kidney beans. They are a great all-round dried bean for keeping in the pantry. Versatile and economical, polenta can be made as a simple, nourishing savoury porridge or set and fried as I have done here. Either way it's a delicious alternative to potatoes, rice or bread. Otherwise serve the Baked Beans as is with Avocado Salsa and Cashew Sour Cream (page 24).*

## Vegan | Gluten free
### Serve 4-6

### Baked Beans
1 cup dried aduki beans, soaked for 24 hours in plenty of water or 400g can cannellini beans
1.2 litres water (to cook dried beans)
1 tablespoon extra-virgin olive oil or rice bran oil
1 tablespoon butter, plant-based or dairy
1 red onion, finely diced
1 stick celery, sliced
2 cloves garlic, crushed
1 capsicum, charred, skinned, deseeded and diced (optional)
700ml jar passata
2–3 tablespoons maple syrup
1 tablespoon cacao powder
1 tablespoon sweet smoked paprika
2 bay leaves
1 tsp salt
1/2 tsp cracked black pepper

### Polenta (Makes 6 cups)
3 tablespoons extra-virgin olive oil
100g butter, plant-based or dairy
1 onion, roughly cut
350g mushrooms, pumpkin or tomato, roughly cut
2 cloves garlic, peeled and roughly chopped
1.4 litres water or liquid vegetable stock for coarse polenta or 1 litre water or liquid vegetable stock for fine polenta
1 tablespoon vegetable bouillon powder (if using water)
2 bay leaves
1 tablespoon fresh thyme or rosemary leaves
1 cup (250g) coarse or fine polenta
1 cup tasty/cheddar cheese, plant-based or dairy, grated
1/2 tsp cracked pepper
1 tsp salt

### Salsa
1 red onion, diced
1 clove garlic, crushed
1 tablespoon red wine vinegar
1 tsp sugar
1 tsp salt
1 cup cherry tomatoes, halved and quartered
1/2 cucumber, diced
1 spring onion or 3 onion weed, sliced
1/2 cup roughly chopped fresh coriander
flesh of 1 avocado, diced
zest and juice of 1 lime or lemon

To make the Baked Beans, drain the beans, then rinse and cover with the water. Bring to the boil and simmer with the lid ajar for 45 minutes, until soft. Remove from the heat, leaving the beans in the water.

Preheat the oven to 180°C. If the casserole dish can go straight on the heat, just put the lid in the oven, otherwise pop the whole dish in to heat.

Place the dish on the stovetop or grab a pan and heat to medium-high. Add the oil and butter. When the butter has melted, sauté the onion, celery, garlic and capsicum. Add the beans, passata, maple syrup, cacao powder, paprika and bay leaves, and stir through.

Transfer to the warmed dish, if needed, put the lid on and bake for 45 minutes, stirring once during this time. Remove from the oven and add the salt and pepper.

To make the Polenta, melt the oil and butter together in a large pot on a medium-high heat. Add the onion, choice of vegetable for flavouring, stock (check amount for the type of polenta using) and herbs. Bring to the boil and simmer for 5 minutes.

Take the pot off the heat and let it cool for a moment. Blend until smooth. Place the pan back on the heat and bring to the boil. Rain in the polenta whilst stirring constantly, you could use a whisk at the start. Cook until it has thickened. It will take 30–45 minutes for the coarse polenta and 15 minutes for the fine polenta.

Lastly, add the cheese and seasoning and stir in. At this point if you want to make the polenta into chips, pour it into a dampened dish or tray about 20 x 30cm and leave undisturbed to set firm. Otherwise serve with the Baked Beans, Avocado Salsa and Cashew Sour Cream (page 24).

To make the Salsa, place the red onion, garlic, vinegar, sugar and salt in a bowl and mix well. Add the tomatoes, cucumber, spring onion and coriander. Stir to combine. Lastly, add the avocado and lime, stir gently and serve.

GLUTEN-FREE BUNS
VERSATILE FAMILY LOAF
PIZZA
GLUTEN-FREE BREAD
GLUTEN-FREE FLATBREADS
HOT CROSS BUNS
GLUTEN-FREE HOT CROSS BUNS
CORNBREAD
SEED CRACKERS
MUESLI BARS - MUESLI

# Baking

# Gluten-free Buns

*These are hands down the best buns ever! They stay soft for days, are easy to make and are full of fabulous dietary fibre, omega-3s plus a heap of other essential nutrients and they taste amazing!*

**Vegan | Gluten free**
**Makes 6–10 buns**

1 cup brown rice flour, sorghum or buckwheat flour
1/2 cup psyllium husk
1/2 cup ground flaxseed
2 tsp yeast
1 tsp molasses or honey
2½ cups warm water
2 tablespoons extra-virgin olive oil
1/2 cup brown rice flour, sorghum or buckwheat
1/2 cup tapioca or potato flour
2 tsp baking powder
1 tsp salt
2 tablespoons soy milk
2 tablespoons sesame or poppy seeds or 1/3 cup cheese, plant-based or dairy, grated

Grease a baking tray. Place the first measurement of flour, psyllium husk, ground flaxseed, yeast, molasses, warm water and olive oil in a mixing bowl. Using a butter knife, mix to combine. Cover with a damp tea towel and leave for 15 minutes.

Add the second measure of flours, baking powder and salt. Mix until it forms a large mass. Knead in the bowl to pick up any excess flour then tip out onto a lightly floured bench. Knead to form a smooth ball.

Cut into six pieces for large buns or 10 pieces for smaller buns. Shape each piece into a round, kneading lightly to form a smooth, flattened ball. Place on a greased tray with 2cm between each bun. Repeat until all are done, cover with a slightly damp tea towel and leave to prove for 30 minutes.

Preheat the oven to 200°C. Remove the tea towel, brush with soy milk and sprinkle each bun with about half a teaspoon of sesame seeds each. Make a deep cut on the top of each bun. Bake for 35 minutes. Remove from the oven and cool on a rack.

# Versatile Family Loaf

This large, white, fluffy bread recipe is my go-to for pizza dough, burger buns or a large family-sized loaf. I love making bread every couple of days for the family, changing it up with the addition of seeds or using half white half wholemeal flour. This recipe is enough for a large loaf, two family-sized pizzas, eight big burger buns, two focaccia breads or two smaller loaves. The added gluten flour helps hold the structure of the loaf so it doesn't collapse as readily while proving. Gluten is the protein in the flour and can be purchased at the supermarket. The flours I use are certified organic, which is really important to me, as non-organic flours contain additives and can be highly processed. Keep the cooled, fresh bread wrapped in a tea towel or in a bread bin, not in the fridge. I save my leftover crusts and put them in an airy place to dry out for a few days, then into a tin to make my own breadcrumbs. You can also dry them out in a low oven. To make breadcrumbs, just break the hard crusts up a bit, put them in the food processor and whizz until you get a fine texture. Keep in an airtight jar.

*Vegan*

*Makes 1 large loaf*

1 tsp yeast
1 tsp honey or other sweetener
4 cups white or wholemeal flour
500ml lukewarm water
1 tsp salt
1 tablespoon extra-virgin olive oil + 1 tablespoon to grease the bowl
2 tablespoons gluten flour (optional)
1 tablespoon fine polenta (optional)

Measure all the ingredients into a mixing bowl. Using a butter knife or dough hook, mix together to form one mass. Tip out and kneed for 5 minutes or let the mixer do the job! Oil the bowl and put the dough back in, cover with a damp tea towel and leave to rise (prove) for 1 1/2–2 hours.

Tip the dough out onto a floured bench. Lightly knead the dough and shape to fit into the loaf tin. Ensure the surface is smooth. (If you want a round loaf, place the dough in a bowl or round proving basket, lined with a flour-dusted tea towel, smooth-side down and cover with the lining tea towel.) Cover with a damp tea towel to prove for another 45 minutes or until it has almost doubled in size.

Preheat the oven to 220°C. If you have used a loaf tin, dust the top of the dough with flour or brush the top with egg wash or soy milk. Score a cut on the top with a sharp knife. If you're making a round loaf, tip the dough out carefully onto a perforated tray, so as not to lose the shape. Score the top with a serrated knife, which helps with rising while cooking. Bake 15 mins for buns and baguettes, 30–40 minutes for a loaf or until it sounds hollow when you tap the bread on the bottom. Cool on a wire rack.

# Pizza

Shape the dough (see Family Loaf) gently with your fingertips, or use a rolling pin to roll it into a thin circle that will fit a round, greased perforated tray.

Preheat the oven to 220–240°C. Place the pizza on the perforated tray, for a super crispy base bake in the oven for 5 minutes or until just starting to bubble and cook then remove and add the sauce and toppings. Cook the pizza for about 15 minutes until the top is golden.

# Pizza Sauce

We have pizza quite often and it's nice to have a sauce ready to go. I love to deepen the flavour by adding flamed-grilled capsicum but you can omit or just finely chop the capsicum and add it to the mix. This makes enough for about four pizzas and will keep in a jar in the fridge for a couple of weeks. Or divide up into clean sterilized jars and cap or small containers and freeze.

## Vegan
## Makes 2 cups

2 tablespoons extra-virgin olive oil
1 red onion, diced
4 cloves garlic, flatten to remove skin
1 capsicum, flame-grilled until the skin is black, remove the skin and seeds and finely chop (optional)
1 tablespoon Balsamic Reduction (page 39) or vinegar
700ml jar passata
1/4 cup water
1 tablespoon roughly chopped oregano, marjoram and rosemary, or dried
1 tsp salt
1/4 tsp black pepper

Place a pan on a medium heat and add the olive oil, onion and garlic. Gently sauté for 5 minutes, moving regularly, until soft and starting to colour. Add the capsicum and balsamic and stir through. Add the passata, water and herbs. Simmer for 25 minutes until thickened. Add the salt and pepper, stir through, then remove from the heat. Spread liberally over the pizza base and store as per instructions in the intro.

## Pizza topping ideas

It's always great to use mozzarella, of course, but Colby cheese is a happy substitute. If you are using plant-based cheese, I find adding it after the sauce, underneath the toppings, has the best result. Here are a few yummy toppings that we make at home.

• Pesto, cauliflower, asparagus, yellow capsicum, cherry tomatoes and olives. Topped with borage, basil, calendula petals, wild mustard or rocket flowers and finely grated Parmesan and avocado with a drizzle of extra-virgin olive oil once it is removed from the oven (as shown).

• Hot roasted pumpkin, mushrooms, tomato and basil sauce topped with tamari roasted seeds.

• Black olive tapenade, potato (roasted or boiled then thinly sliced), cherry tomatoes. After the pizza comes out of the oven, top with slices of Brie and fresh thyme.

• Broccoli, roasted pumpkin, fresh figs, blue cheese, olives and walnuts.

# Gluten-free Bread

*Perfecting a gluten-free loaf has been a long-time ambition for me and I'm proud to share that I have finally cracked it! Here are two versions, one for the seedy lovers and a plain version. Soft and fluffy, this loaf is perfect for sandwiches. The seedy version makes a delightful nutty toast (I like to slice it thinly). It will last and stay soft for more than four days in a bread bin. It is also a one bowl, that needs only one prove and minimal equipment. Even the kids can make it! You can also use this recipe for making pizza bases.*

## Vegan | Gluten free
## Makes a 12 x 22cm loaf

### Seed version

2 tsp yeast
1 tsp sugar or honey
1/3 cup psyllium husk
1/4 cup flaxseeds
1/4 cup chia seeds
1/4 cup sunflower or pumpkin seeds
2 cups lukewarm water
1/4 cup soy milk
1 tablespoon extra-virgin olive oil or hemp oil + 1 tsp for the tin
3/4 cup brown rice flour
3/4 cup tapioca or potato starch/flour
3/4 cup sorghum, buckwheat or cornmeal
1 tsp salt
1 tablespoon sesame seeds

### Plain version

2 tsp yeast
1 tsp honey or sugar
1/3 cup psyllium husk
1/3 cup ground flaxseed
2 cups lukewarm water
1/4 cup soy milk
1 tablespoon extra-virgin olive oil or hemp oil + 1 tsp to grease the tin
1 cup brown rice flour
1 cup tapioca or potato flour
1 cup sorghum, buckwheat or cornmeal
1 tsp salt

Grease the loaf tin. Measure the yeast, honey, psyllium, flaxseed, chia seeds (if using), sunflower seeds (if using), warm water and soy milk into a bowl. Using a butter knife mix to combine.

Add the olive oil, brown rice flour, tapioca flour, sorghum flour and salt. Mix until it forms one mass, or near to it, then tip out onto the bench and kneed to form a smooth round. Place the sesame seeds on the bench and roll the top of the dough over to pick up the sesame seeds. Shape into a loaf.

Place in the tin, sesame-side up, and cover with a damp tea towel. Leave to prove for 2 hours. Preheat the oven to 220°C.

Remove the tea towel and fan bake for 45 minutes–1 hour. Tap to check if it sounds hollow, remove from the tin and cool on a rack.

# Gluten-free Flatbreads

*These flat breads were a revelation! They are soft and pliable, ready to wrap any tasty filling you can think of. They keep well for a day in an in an airtight container, beeswax wrap or cling film – and keep out of the fridge.*

*Vegan | Gluten free*

*Makes 12*

2 tsp yeast
1/3 cup psyllium husk
1/4 cup flaxseed, ground or whole
1 1/2 cup warm water
1 tablespoon extra-virgin olive oil or hemp seed oil
1/2 cup sorghum flour or buckwheat flour
1/2 cup brown rice flour
1/2 cup tapioca or potato flour
1 tsp salt
1/4 cup extra-virgin olive oil

Measure the yeast, psyllium husk, flaxseed, warm water and oil into a bowl and stir together using a butter knife. Add the flours and salt and stir through thoroughly.

Using your hands, press and knead into a dough. When it's all sticking together, tip out onto the bench and knead until smooth.

Preheat a hot plate (if using). Divide into 12 pieces, roll each out into a ball then roll out to 3mm thickness, repeat for all. Heat a cast-iron pan (or hot plate) on a high temperature. Add 1 teaspoon of oil per flatbread and cook on each side for 45 seconds and add another teaspoon of oil to the pan before flipping to cook the other side.

Stack on a plate or board covered with a tea towel. Cover the flatbreads while making the next one. Repeat until done.

# Hot Cross Buns

My favourite thing to eat at Easter time is hot cross buns: soft and spicy, moist and delicious, the perfect start to a good Friday! When I make breads with dried yeast I like to bloom the yeast with the flour, water and sweetener for the first ferment to develop flavour. I also find this helps with the general rise of the bread as the yeasts are nice and active when they come into contact with the spices, which can limit the dough rising if too much is added. But you can also miss this step out and just throw it all in at once.

This recipe is refined sugar free and the sweetener's used to give the buns a delicious flavour and improved texture. Maltexo is a barley-based malt extract which some may remember from childhood, I love the flavour but you could also use golden syrup or honey, if that is what you have in the pantry. I use a mixer with a dough hook attachment, but you can use a butter knife and your hands and knead the dough, if you don't have one.

I use a damp tea towel instead of plastic wrap when proving, but you might like to cover this with a bee's wax wrap to help keep all the moisture in that you can. This helps create the ideal environment for the yeast to thrive, as well as the ambient temperature being around 20–25°C. If you like soft hot cross buns, I recommend using a roasting tray with sides to bake the buns in. This recipe also makes a great fruit loaf, if you fancy it.

## Vegan
## Makes 12 buns or 1 loaf

2 tsp dried yeast
1/4 cup honey, maple syrup or Maltexo
1 cup white high-grade flour
1 cup lukewarm water, whey, almond or soy milk
1 cup white high-grade flour or plain white flour with
1 tablespoon gluten flour
1 cup wholemeal or rye flour
1/4 cup Dutch cocoa (optional)
1 tsp ground cinnamon
1 tsp mixed spice
1/2 tsp salt
1 cup raisins, sultanas, cranberries and/or diced apricots or dates
50g butter, dairy or plant-based, melted
1 heaped tablespoon flour
1 heaped tsp cornflour or custard powder
1 1/2 tablespoons water or milk
2 tablespoons runny honey or jam or marmalade, thinned by adding 1 tsp boiling water and stir until smooth

Place the yeast, honey, first measure of flour and water in a mixing bowl. Mix well and leave to prove (bloom), covered with a damp tea towel, for 1 hour.

Remove the tea towel and add the second measures of flour, cocoa (if using), spices, salt, dried fruit and butter. Mix well with a dough hook on a medium speed for 5 minutes. Prove for about 1 hour, covered with a damp tea towel, until doubled in size.

Butter a 20 x 30 cm roasting tray. Tip the dough out onto a floured surface. Cut the dough in half, then each half into six. Shape into balls, tucking the ugly ends underneath so you have a nice smooth top. Place the buns in lines of three across by four lengthways. Cover with a damp tea towel and prove (rise) for 1 hour, until doubled in size.

Preheat the oven to 200°C. In a small bowl, mix together the last measurement of flour, cornflour and water. Stir together until smooth. Use a teaspoon to carefully pour lines lengthways in one smooth motion from one end to the other. Repeat widthways over each bun. You could also use a piping bag.

Bake for 30 minutes until golden brown. Transfer the buns to a cooling rack and immediately brush the tops with the honey.

# Gluten-free Hot Cross Buns

*Vegan | Gluten free*
*Makes 9 buns*

2 tsp yeast
1/4 cup coconut sugar
1 cup sorghum flour, brown rice or buckwheat flour
(use a different flour for the second measure)
1/2 cup psyllium husk
1/2 cup ground flaxseed
2 1/2 cups warm plant milk
2 tablespoons maple syrup, brown rice malt syrup,
molasses or honey
2 tsp ground cinnamon
2 tsp mixed spice
1 tsp ginger
1 cup raisins, cranberries or chopped apricots
zest and juice 1 of orange
1/4 cup coconut oil, melted (use the left over oil for
greasing the tins)
1/2 cup sorghum flour, brown rice or buckwheat flour
1/2 cup tapioca flour (or 1/4 cup, if using cocoa)
1/4 cup Dutch cocoa (optional)
2 tsp baking powder
1 tsp salt
1 tablespoon rice flour
1 heaped tablespoon cornflour
1 1/2 tablespoons water
2 tablespoons runny honey or jam or marmalade,
warmed by adding 1 tsp boiling water and stir until
smooth

Measure the yeast, coconut sugar, first measurement of flour, psyllium husk, flaxseed and milk into a mixing bowl. Using a butter knife, mix to combine. Cover with a damp tea towel and leave in a warm place for 15 minutes.

Add the maple syrup, cinnamon, mixed spice, ginger, dried fruit, orange zest and juice, coconut oil, second measure of flour, tapioca flour, Dutch cocoa (if using), baking powder and salt. Mix until it forms a large mass. Knead in the bowl to pick up any excess flour then tip out onto a lightly rice-floured bench. Knead to form a smooth ball then cut into nine pieces. Form each piece into a round bun shape, kneading lightly to form a smooth ball. Place on a greased roasting tray. Cover with a damp tea towel and leave in a warm place for 40–50 minutes. Preheat the oven to 200°C.

Make the cross mixture by mixing the rice flour, cornflour and water together in a small bowl until smooth. Use a teaspoon to carefully pour lines lengthways in one smooth motion from one end to the other. Repeat widthways over each bun. You could also use a piping bag.

Bake for 35 minutes until golden brown. Remove the buns from the oven, release the sides with a spatula and tip onto a cooling rack. Carefully flip them over and brush the tops with your chosen syrup.

# Cornbread

*Warm cornbread straight from the oven is hard to beat. Cooking it in a cast-iron pan ensures it cooks evenly and doesn't have a chance to dry out, as well as giving it a crispy crust and moist interior. If you don't have a cast-iron pan, you will need an ovenproof pan or dish that you can heat on the element first before baking. If you choose the oil option, the pan still needs to be heated before adding the batter. Soaking the polenta beforehand gives it a chance to start absorbing some liquid which is essential to achieving moist cornbread.*

## Vegan | Gluten free
## Makes a 25cm round

1 1/2 cup fine polenta
2 cups milk, plant-based or dairy
1 1/2 cup grated cheese, plant-based or dairy
1 cup sweetcorn kernals, fresh, frozen or tinned
1 egg (or 1 tablespoon ground flaxseed mixed with 1/4 cup water)
1 tsp baking powder
1 tsp baking soda
2 tablespoons cornflour or potato flour
1 tsp salt
1/4 tsp cracked black pepper
50g butter, extra-virgin olive oil or rice bran oil
1 tomato, thinly sliced

Mix the polenta and milk together, set aside to soak for 15 minutes, stirring twice during this time.

Preheat the oven to 200°C. Add the cheese, sweetcorn, egg, baking powder, baking soda, cornflour, salt and pepper and mix to combine. Place the cast-iron or ovenproof pan on a high heat and melt the butter. Pour the batter into the pan and top with tomato slices.

Bake for 25 minutes. The bread should be pulling from the sides and golden brown. Serve immediately.

Cornbread

# Seed Crackers

*These crackers are really easy to make and full of nutrients – and you know there are no nasties added to homemade crackers. Any combination of seeds can be used, just ensure the correct amount of chia and/or flaxseeds are added as these hold the crackers together. You can make them savoury or sweet, so they are great for the lunchbox or as a snack to keep you going in between meals. We had almond butter with our last batch of sweet ones – delicious!*

Vegan | Gluten free
Makes 30

## Savoury version

1/4 cup sesame seeds
1/4 cup flaxseeds
1/4 cup hemp hearts
1/2 cup chia seeds
1/2 cup sunflower seeds, finely chopped (optional)
1/2 cup pumpkin seeds, finely chopped (optional)
1 cup water
1 tablespoon light soy sauce, tamari or coconut aminos
1 clove garlic, crushed
1 tablespoon chopped or dried rosemary, thyme or oregano
1 tsp Himalayan salt

## Sweet version

1 banana, mashed with a fork
1/4 cup chia seeds
1/4 cup flaxseeds
1/4 cup hemp hearts
1/4 cup sesame seeds
1/4 cup maple syrup
1/2 cup sunflower seeds, finely chopped
1/2 cup pumpkin seeds, finely chopped
1/2 cup coconut thread
3/4 cup water

Measure the sesame seeds, flaxseeds, hemp hearts, chia seeds, sunflower seeds (if using), pumpkin seeds (if using), water, soy sauce, garlic and herbs into a bowl. Mix then leave to sit for 5–10 minutes, until there is no pool of liquid at the bottom. Stir a few times to help absorption.

Preheat the oven to 150°C and line a tray with baking paper. Using a spatula spread the seed mix out onto the baking paper evenly. Then place another sheet of baking paper over the top of the mix. Use a rolling pin to flatten evenly. Remove the paper and sprinkle the salt over the top.

Bake for 30 minutes, then take it out of the oven and flip it onto a separate sheet of baking paper. To do this, use another similar-sized tray with a piece of baking paper on it, sandwich and flip both trays together. Slice into pieces with a pizza roller or knife, then bake for a further 30 minutes until dried and crispy. If you are concerned that it is not dry enough, turn the oven off and leave it to cool in the oven.

# Muesli Bars

*These quick, easy, nutritious muesli bars are great for lunch boxes or as a quick breakfast bar before running out of the house on frantic mornings. Dark chocolate is high in iron, minerals and is a powerful source of antioxidants. It also makes them look very appetizing.*

## Vegan | Gluten free
## Makes 24

2 tablespoons chia seeds
1/2 cup water
5 cups muesli or granola
1/3 cup honey, maple syrup, date syrup or Maltexo
1/2 cup tahini or nut butter of choice
2 tablespoons coconut oil, melted
1/2 tsp salt
150g dark chocolate (optional)
a pinch of flaky sea salt (optional)

Preheat the oven to 175°C. Line an 18 x 28cm tin with baking paper. Measure the chia seeds and water into a bowl, stir and leave to absorb.

Meanwhile, measure the muesli or granola, sweetener, tahini and salt into a bowl. Add the chia mixture and mix well to combine. Tip into the prepared tin and push down evenly. Bake for 10–15 minutes.

Remove from the oven and cool in the tin. Once cold, slice into bars. The bars can be stored as is or topped with chocolate. Keeping the chocolate in the packet, smash it up on the bench (with a rolling pin) until well broken up. Tip two-thirds of the chocolate into a heatproof bowl placed over a pot of simmering water, stirring occasionally. Make sure the bowl doesn't touch the water. When the chocolate has melted, take it off the heat and add the rest of the chocolate and stir until it's all melted. Use a teaspoon to generously drizzle the chocolate over the bars in a zig-zag pattern. Sprinkle with salt (if using). Leave to set for 10–15 minutes. Store in an airtight container or tin.

## Muesli
## Vegan
## Makes 1.5 kg

8 cups rolled or regular oats
1/3 cup coconut, desiccated or thread
1/2 cup pumpkin seeds, roughly chopped
1/2 cup amaranth puffs or other puffed grains
1/3 cup coconut oil
1/3 cup apple or orange juice or kombucha
1/3 cup honey, maple syrup or Maltexo
2 cups preferred dried fruits (e.g. raisins, apricots, cranberries, dates)
1 cup LSA (a blend of ground linseeds, sunflower seeds and almonds)
1/2 cup hemp seeds

Preheat the oven to 150°C. I make this in the two biggest roasting pans I have. You need room to move everything around so it toasts easily. Grease these with a little coconut oil then pour in the oats, coconut and pumpkin seeds. Bake for 10 minutes.

Meanwhile, place the coconut oil, juice (or kombucha) and preferred sweetener in a small pot. Heat together gently until just melted.

Remove the oats from the oven and add the liquid mixture to the tray and stir well until everything is well coated. Return to the oven for about 30 minutes until dry and starting to toast, stir every 10 minutes to make sure it all toasts evenly. Remove the tray from the oven and cool.

Measure out the dried fruit into a bowl and add the LSA and hemp seeds, stir together then place half of this mix in the food processor. Pulse together until roughly chopped. Add to the oat mix, stir and leave to cool completely.

Store in an airtight cereal container or jar.

ORANGE CHOCOLATE AND ALMOND CAKE WITH
WHIPPED CHOCOLATE GANACHE

SUMMER FRUITS ICE CREAM

HONEY CRACKLES

BERRY CHOCOLATE DESSERT CAKE

LEMON CHIA CAKE

CHOCOLATE CHERRY MUD CAKE

CHOCOLATE AVOCADO SLICE

TAMARILLO AND QUINCE BAKED CHEESECAKE

GINGER LOAF WITH MAPLE WALNUT BUTTER FROSTING

SPICED CUTTER BISCUITS

HEMP 'N' RAISIN THUMB PRINT COOKIES

NUTTY CHOCOLATE CRISPY COOKIES

BROWN SUGAR SHORTBREAD

PEACH CRUMBLE SLICE

FRUITY FRANGIPANE TART

KUMARA PIE WITH GINGERNUT CRUST

# Sweets

# Orange, Hazelnut and Almond Cake with Whipped Chocolate Ganache

*This is like a pudding cake – dense and moist. It also happens to be one of my all-time favourite cakes. You can make it as a regular cake or divide the mixture between two tins and spread the ganache between the layers. For this picture, I doubled the recipe for a special occasion big birthday cake. A mini food processor is the best way to achieve a nice fine-breadcrumb texture for the hazelnuts.*

*Chocolate ganache is the ultimate versatile icing. The consistency can easily be changed, and it firms up once cold. You can pour it over the cake for a smooth finish or wait until it cools for a more textured look. You can also whip ganache once cold for an airy texture and lighter colour which is what I've done here.*

## Vegan | Gluten free
### Makes a 26cm cake or divide between 2 x 26cm tins to layer

2 oranges, tangelos or 3 mandarins
250g unrefined sugar
4 eggs
1 1/2 cups ground almonds
1 cup hazelnuts, ground in the food processor until resembling fine breadcrumbs
2 tablespoons baking powder
freeze-dried mandarins or crystallized citrus peel, to decorate

## Vegan option
Replace eggs with:
2 tablespoons ground flaxseed mixed with 1/4 cup orange cooking water
1/2 cup brown rice flour

## Whipped Ganache
400ml cream, coconut or dairy
250g dark chocolate, broken up well

Prepare the oranges a little in advance. Place the whole oranges in a pot and cover well with water. Bring to the boil, then turn down to simmer for about 1 hour, until the oranges are soft. Drain (reserve 1/4 cup of the water if you are making the egg-free version) and leave to cool for 10 minutes.

Preheat the oven to 160°C and line a 26cm cake tin. When the oranges are cool enough to handle, pull them apart and remove any pips and stringy pith. Put the oranges in a food processor and blitz until very smooth.

If you are making the egg-free version, mix the ground flaxseed and reserved orange cooking liquid and leave to absorb for 10 minutes.

Measure the sugar, eggs (or absorbed flax egg) and brown rice flour into a large bowl and whisk together well. Add the orange purée, ground almonds, ground hazelnuts and baking powder and whisk everything together well. Scrape into the prepared tin.

Bake for 50–60 minutes for the one tin cake or 30 minutes if you have divided it into two. The cake is ready when you insert a skewer and it comes out clean. Cool in the tin for 10 minutes, then take the cake out of the tin and cool completely on a rack.

Meanwhile, make the Whipped Ganache. Pour the cream into a pot and gently warm on a medium-high heat, stirring frequently, until it is just coming to the boil. Then immediately pour on top of the chocolate in a heatproof bowl. Leave for 1 minute then stir together until smooth. Pour through a sieve to completely remove any lumps and leave to cool completely in the fridge before whipping. When the ganache is cold, whip on a medium speed and slowly increase to high speed. When it starts to thicken, reduce the speed. Be careful not to over whip as it will become grainy.

Remove the paper from the cake and transfer to a plate or cake board. If layering, you could spread the first layer of cake with marmalade or go straight ahead with a layer of ganache. Evenly spread right to the edges, an offset spatula is easiest to use for this. Then carefully place the second layer on top and press down in the centre lightly to make sure it is flat and even. Spoon the remaining ganache on top of the cake and, using a warmed spatula, smooth the ganache over the top first then gradually make your way around the sides until you have a smooth, even finish.

Lastly, if you want to get a 'drip cake' look, make up half a recipe of ganache, cool then pour slowly around the edges creating the drips then pour in the centre top of the cake to puddle, careful not to pour too much at this stage or it will overflow, ruining your drips. Leave to cool completely and set. Top with freeze-dried mandarins or crystallized citrus peel.

# Summer Fruits Ice Cream

It wouldn't be summer without the need for ice cream to cool us down a bit. This Philadelphia-style ice cream doesn't use eggs to make a custard, instead it is thickened with fruit. Of course, an ice-cream machine will churn this perfectly, but you can stir the ice cream while it's freezing to create almost the same effect. Homemade ice cream always benefits from being left out of the freezer for 10 minutes before serving.

Makes 1 litre

Vegan | Gluten free

4 cups (500g) strawberries, other berries, or stone fruit, cleaned of stalks or pips
100ml water
zest and juice of 1/2 a lemon
1 vanilla pod or 1 tsp vanilla paste
1/2 cup (125g) sugar
300ml cream, coconut or dairy

Measure the berries, water, lemon zest and juice and vanilla into a pot and simmer for 5 minutes, until soft. Add the sugar and stir to dissolve.

Cool for 10 minutes, then add the cream. Blend until smooth and cool. When cold, churn in an ice-cream machine or pour into a freezer-proof container. Stir every 30 minutes until frozen.

# Honey Crackles

Not just a party treat, these yummy honey crackles are fantastic for lunch boxes. With the added nutritious goodies of chia, sesame seeds, amaranth, quinoa and/or millet they are sure to please adults and children alike.

*Makes 24 bars*

*Vegan | Gluten free*

**3 cups rice puffs**
**1 cup millet, amaranth or quinoa puffs**
**1/4 cup chia seeds**
**1/4 cup sesame seeds**
**3/4 cup desiccated coconut**
**1/2 cup butter, plant-based or dairy or 1/2 cup coconut oil + a pinch of salt**
**1/3 cup honey**
**1/2 cup unrefined sugar**

Line a 30 x 20cm slice tin. Measure the puffs, seeds and coconut into a large bowl and set aside.

Measure the butter, honey and sugar into a pot and melt together on a medium-high heat, while stirring gently. Bring to a steady boil for 3 minutes.

Working quickly, pour the bubbling mix into the bowl with the puffs and mix well. Scrape into the lined tin and press down flat as you can with the back of a spatula. To get it really flat I like to then go over it with one of the kid's mini rolling pins.

Leave to cool in the tin, then cut into bars before it's completely cold. Store in a baking tin or an airtight container.

# Berry Chocolate Dessert Cake

*This is like a frozen cheesecake or ice cream cake but without any dairy or cheese involved. It is great because you can make it a couple of days ahead of time. Transfer it from the freezer to the fridge an hour before serving, so that it has a chance to defrost slightly. Note that the nuts and maybe the dates will need to be well soaked before making this recipe. Use hot water to soak cashew nuts, if short on time.*

*Vegan | Gluten free*

*Makes a 20cm cake*

1 cup macadamia nuts or almonds
1 tsp macadamia or coconut oil
1/2 cup desiccated coconut
1/4 cup Dutch cocoa or raw cacao powder
a pinch of salt flakes or pink salt
1/2 cup date purée or medjool dates, pitted (or regular dates pre-soaked for 10-20 minutes in warm water)
3/4 cup virgin coconut oil, melted
2 tablespoons cacao butter, melted
2 1/2 cup (350g) raw cashew nuts, soaked for at least 2 hours
1 cup coconut cream
zest and juice of 1 lemon
1/2 cup coconut nectar or maple syrup
1–2 tsp vanilla paste
3 cups fresh berries

Place the macadamia nuts, oil, coconut, cocoa, salt and date in a food processor with the chopping blade fitted. Blitz until it all comes together in one mass and is chopped well. You may need to give the food processor a jig or scrape down to help it blend evenly. Tip out into a cling film-lined springform tin and push the mixture down evenly with a spatula or your hands. Chill in the freezer while you make the filling. You will need to clean out your food processor.

In a pot, gently melt the coconut oil and cacao butter together. Measure the cashew nuts into the food processor, along with the melted mixture, coconut cream, lemon zest and juice, coconut nectar, vanilla and berries. Blitz until super smooth and creamy, about 5 minutes. Scrape the filling onto the chilled base and smooth out evenly. Return to the freezer, cover with cling film and freeze for at least 6 hours.

Remove from the freezer and carefully push the cake up and out of the tin. Remove the cling film and place the cake on a plate in the fridge for 1 hour before serving. Top with fresh berries to serve.

# Lemon Chia Cake

*An adaptation of lemon poppy seed cake, with the addition of chia seeds which are a fantastic egg substitute as well as a powerhouse of nutrients. Pair with ice cream for a dessert or you can also make this into a celebration cake with beautiful fruity frosting.*

*For the Coconut Frosting, the coconut oil will need to be just soft. If runny, pop it in the fridge for a bit. You can add colour and flavour to the frosting by mixing in your choice of freeze-dried berry powder. I love raspberry and lemon together.*

## Vegan | Gluten free
## Makes a 22cm cake

2 tablespoons desiccated coconut
2 tablespoons chia seeds
1/3 cup water
1 1/2 cups plain flour or 3/4 cup brown rice flour
4 tsp baking powder
1/2 cup desiccated coconut
3/4 cup unrefined cane sugar
90g virgin coconut oil, soft or melted
1 1/2 cups soy, almond or coconut milk
zest and juice of 2 lemons or limes

### Gluten-free option

Replace flour with:
3/4 cup cornflour
2 tablespoons coconut flour

### Coconut Frosting

1 cup coconut oil, virgin or refined
1 cup icing sugar
2 tablespoons lemon or lime juice
1–2 tsp boiling water or 1 tablespoon freeze-dried berry powder mixed with 1 tablespoon boiling water

Preheat the oven to 180°C. Grease a 22cm cake tin well with coconut oil. Place the first measure of coconut in the tin and gently shake the tin to move it around so it goes up the sides and covers the base well.

In a small bowl, soak the chia seeds in the water for 5 minutes, stirring twice during this time.

Sieve the flour and baking powder into a large mixing bowl, then add the second measure of coconut and sugar. Make a well in the centre and add the coconut oil, milk, citrus and chia mixture. Whisk together until just smooth and pour into the prepared tin.

Bake for 50–60 minutes. It is done when an inserted skewer comes out clean. Cool for a few minutes in the tin, then tip onto a rack to cool completely.

To make the Coconut Frosting, measure the coconut oil, icing sugar and lemon juice into a mixing bowl. Whisk on high speed, adding the water or berry mix a little at a time until smooth and whipped. Spread or pipe onto the cake once cold.

# Chocolate Cherry Mud Cake

*This cake is decadent! Cherry and chocolate is one of the best combinations and, with coconut added to the mix, it's to die for. No one will even know that it's vegan and gluten-free. Dutch cocoa has a superior dark colour and adds moisture to the mix but if you don't have it just use regular cocoa or raw cacao. The topping can be used as an icing or chocolate sauce.*

## Vegan | Gluten free
## Makes a 21cm cake

200g dates
1 tsp baking soda
100g dark chocolate, chopped
1 cup coconut oil, virgin or refined
1/2 cup boiling water
1/2 cup Dutch cocoa
1/2 cup desiccated coconut
1/2 cup wholemeal flour, wholemeal spelt or coconut flour
1/2 cup coconut sugar
2 tablespoons maple syrup
2 tsp baking powder
3 eggs (or 3 tablespoons chia seeds mixed with 3/4 cup water and left to absorb for 5 minutes)
250g cherries, pitted (1/2 in mix, 1/2 on top)

## Icing or Sauce

1/3 cup coconut oil, virgin or refined
1/2 cup cacao powder
2 tablespoons cacao butter
3 tablespoons coconut nectar, maple or agave syrup
1 tsp vanilla extract
100g dark chocolate, chopped

Preheat the oven to 180°C and line a 21 cm cake tin with baking paper. In a bowl, combine the dates, baking soda, chocolate, coconut oil and boiling water. Stir and leave to melt.

Measure the cocoa, coconut, flour, sugar, maple syrup and baking powder into another bowl. Transfer the date chocolate mixture to a food processor and whizz until smooth. Stir into the dry mix bowl along with the chia mix or egg and half of the cherries. Mix together and scrape into a lined tin, then scatter the remaining cherries on the top.

Bake for 1 hour until an inserted skewer comes out clean. Remove from the tin and cool on a cooling rack.

To make the Icing, measure the coconut oil, cacao powder, cacao butter, sweetener, vanilla and chocolate into a small pot. Melt gently on a low heat, stirring all the time, and remove as soon as it has melted.

Pour through a sieve into a jug. Use the back of a spatula to push the mixture through. This helps give a smooth texture to the icing/sauce.

Pour over the cake when cool or use as a sauce.

# Chocolate Avocado Slice

*This was the first raw treat I made and I fell in love with it. It's rich and decadent but full of goodness. A great sweet treat that you can keep in the freezer for a month or in the fridge for a week (if it lasts that long!). Adding one or two drops of essential oils such as orange or lime takes this delicious treat to the next level but is totally optional. You could also use the zest of an orange or lime to flavour, if preferred. If you're having a get-together, this is a great tart to make a few days in advance, as you can keep it in the freezer until you need it. Remember to take it out of the freezer at least 1 hour before you serve it.*

### Vegan | Gluten free
### Makes 16 pieces

200g whole almonds or hazelnuts
1/4 tsp Himalayan or flaked sea salt
200g Medjool dates, stones removed or date paste
flesh of 3 medium avocados
1 cup coconut oil, virgin or refined
1 tsp vanilla bean paste or 1 vanilla pod, seeds only
1–2 drops food-grade essential oils or citrus zest (optional)
2 cups raw cacao powder
1/2 cup coconut sugar
1/2 cup maple or date syrup

Line a 20 x 30cm tin with baking paper. Make the base first: measure the almonds, salt and dates into a food processor. Blitz until it starts to stick together. Tip into the tin and push it down as evenly as you can, right to the edges, then put the tin in the freezer to set while you make the topping.

Rinse out the food processor, put it back together, then add the avocados, coconut oil, vanilla, essential oils (if using), cacao powder, sugar and syrup. Blitz well until completely smooth. (Be careful not to let the machine get hot, as this will split the filling.)

Take the tin out of the freezer and pour the topping onto the base, smoothing it evenly. I drag a fork over the top to create a bit of texture. Put the tin back in the freezer for at least 3 hours. Transfer it to an airtight container and keep it in the fridge.

# Tamarillo and Quince Baked Cheesecake

*This baked cheesecake is one I have been making for years and years. The homemade biscuit base means you don't need to buy premade biscuits. The topping options are endless; this simple fruit purée makes the most of seasonal fruit. I use my electric mixer to make this cake, as you need to beat the egg and sugar for a good while to get it light and airy, you could also use an electric hand beater. For the vegan version you will need a food processor.*

## Vegan | Gluten free | Makes a large 26cm cake

### Base

175g butter, plant-based or dairy
1/2 cup unrefined cane sugar
1 cup plain flour
1/3 cup cornflour
3/4 cup macadamia nuts, coarsely ground

### Filling

300g cream cheese, at room temperature
250g ricotta
1/4 cup liquid honey or maple syrup
6 eggs
1/2 cup unrefined cane sugar
1 tsp vanilla paste
2 tablespoons cornflour + 2 tablespoons water, mixed until smooth

### Vegan Base

175g butter, plant-based
1/2 cup unrefined cane sugar
1/2 cup brown rice flour
3/4 cup macadamia nuts, coarsely ground
1/2 cup cornflour
1/4 cup coconut flour

### Vegan Filling

2 x 300g blocks tofu
1 cup coconut cream
1 tsp baking powder
1/4 cup liquid honey or maple syrup
1 tsp vanilla paste

### Topping

2 quinces, peeled and cut into small pieces
juice and zest of 1 lemon
flesh of 3 tamarillos
1 cup unrefined cane sugar

Line a springform cake tin with baking paper. Preheat the oven to 160°C. Measure the butter and first measure of sugar into a mixer and cream together, using the paddle attachment. Add the flours and macadamia nuts and mix on a slow speed until it starts to stick together.

Push into the lined tin evenly, prick with a fork and bake for 15 minutes while you make the filling. Remove the base from the oven. It should be set on the top but not coloured.

Meanwhile, clean the bowl and paddle, then re-assemble the mixer. Place the cream cheese, ricotta and honey in the mixer bowl and beat together until smooth. Scrape into a large bowl. Change to the whisk attachment and add the eggs, second measure of sugar and vanilla to the mixer. Whisk on a medium-high speed until light and fluffy, about 10 minutes. Add half of the egg mixture to the cheese mixture and whisk until smooth, then add the remaining egg mixture along with the cornflour mixture and fold through gently. Pour into the tin and return to the oven.

For the vegan option, add the tofu and coconut cream, baking powder, sweetener and vanilla to a food processor and blitz until smooth. Add the cornflour mixture and blitz until combined. Pour into the tin and return to the oven. Bake for 1 hour 40 minutes. It should be set but still have a little wobble. When the cheesecake is cold, place in the fridge to chill. This is essential for the base to firm up completely before removing from the tin.

Remove the outside part of the springform tin, leaving the base on. Transfer the cheesecake to a serving plate. Top with the cooled topping.

To make the topping, place the quince, lemon, tamarillos and sugar in a pot and stir to combine. Bring to the boil, then turn down to a simmer. Cook for 10 minutes. Remove from the heat and leave to cool. Blitz into a purée or mash well.

# Ginger Loaf with Maple Walnut Butter Frosting

*Moist, sweet and spicy, this loaf was one of my first vegan baking favourites. The molasses gives the loaf a lovely rich colour and intense flavour, which I adore. I haven't been able to access molasses for a year or so, so here I have substituted with golden syrup. Date syrup is readily available at supermarkets and is super cost effective, compared to real maple syrup. It is essential to let the walnut butter cool before adding the coconut oil for the frosting. To firm up soft or melted coconut oil, pop it in the fridge until firm but not completely solid before using.*

## Vegan | Gluten free
### Makes a 12 x 22 cm loaf

1 cup wholemeal flour
1 cup plain flour
2 tsp baking powder
1 tsp baking soda
small pinch of salt
1 heaped tablespoon ground ginger
1 tsp mixed spice
1 tsp ground cinnamon
1/2 cup rice bran oil or other neutral flavoured oil
1/2 cup maple or date syrup
1/2 cup molasses or golden syrup
1 cup milk, plant-based or dairy
1 tablespoon apple cider vinegar
1 tsp vanilla extract

### Gluten-free option

Replace flour with:
1 cup almond meal
1/3 cup coconut flour, brown rice or sorghum
1/3 cup cornflour
1 tablespoon ground flaxseed

### Walnut Butter Frosting

1/2 cup walnuts + extra to decorate
1/4 cup maple syrup
1/4 cup coconut oil, virgin or refined, not melted

Line the tin with baking paper. Preheat the oven to 160°C. Sift the flours, baking powder, baking soda, salt and spices into a large bowl.

In a separate bowl, measure in the oil, syrups, milk, vinegar and vanilla and whisk to emulsify. Make a well in the centre of the dry ingredients and pour in the wet ingredients, then whisk together. The mixture will be quite wet.

Pour into the loaf tin and bake for 1 hour. It's done when an inserted skewer comes out clean. Cool on a rack. I keep the baking paper on so it's easy to transfer to a tin or airtight container when completely cold.

To make the Walnut Butter Frosting, place the walnuts and maple syrup in a food processor and whizz together until a butter forms. Add the coconut oil and whizz until combined. Spread over the top of the loaf and sprinkle with walnuts.

# Spiced Cutter Biscuits

The kids will love helping to make these. It is a lovely dough to roll with a delicate spice and honey taste. The easiest way to make this is in a mixer with a paddle attachment. Alternatively, use a large bowl and a wooden spoon.

## Vegan | Gluten free
## Makes 30

250g butter, plant-based or dairy, softened
3/4 cup unrefined cane sugar
1/4 cup honey or brown rice syrup
1 egg (or 1 tablespoon flaxseed mixed with 1/4 cup water + 2 tablespoons plant milk)
1 tsp vanilla extract
1 tsp cinnamon or mixed spice
1 1/2 cups flour
1 1/2 cups wholemeal spelt or plain flour
1/4 tsp baking soda

### Gluten-free option
Replace flours with:
1/2 cup brown rice flour
1/2 cup tapioca flour
1/2 cup cornflour
1/4 tsp guar gum
1/2 cup soy milk

Line one or two flat baking trays with baking paper. Preheat the oven to 175°C. In a mixing bowl, cream together the butter, sugar and honey until pale, using a paddle attachment. Add the egg, vanilla, spice, flour and baking soda and mix until it all comes together.

Tip onto the bench and knead lightly, then cover with a damp tea towel and set aside for 30 minutes.

Roll out dough to 5mm thick, then use cookie cutters to cut out shapes. Transfer to the baking tray/s and bake for 10–15 minutes, until just golden.

Cool slightly on the tray before transferring to a cooling rack to cool completely. Store in an airtight tin.

# Hemp 'n' Raisin Thumb Print Cookies

These cookies are not only cute and easy to make they are also healthy! With omega-3 and magnesium-rich hemp hearts plus sweet bursts of raisins which are high in iron and minerals, these little tin fillers will keep everyone happy. For the gluten-free version measure the flours lightly by scooping and shaking sideways so you just get scant cups.

## Vegan | Gluten free
## Makes 15

120g butter, plant-based or dairy, softened
1/3 cup coconut sugar
1 tablespoon hempseed oil
2 tablespoons brown rice, date or golden syrup
2 cups wholemeal flour, oat flour or 1 1/2 cups sorghum flour
1/2 cup cornflour, tapioca or potato flour
1/2 cup raisins
1/3 cup hemp hearts
1 tsp ground cinnamon
1 tsp vanilla paste
1/2 tsp baking soda

Line a baking tray with baking paper and preheat the oven to 180°C. Measure the butter and coconut sugar into a mixing bowl. Using the paddle attachment or a wooden spoon, cream until pale. Add the hempseed oil, syrup, flour, raisins, hemp hearts, cinnamon, vanilla and baking soda and mix until combined.

Scoop tablespoon-sized portions into your hands, roll into a flat round, then place on the tray and push down in the centre with your thumb.

Bake for 10 minutes, remove from the oven and cool on a rack.

Spiced Cutter Cookies

Hemp 'n' Raisin Thumb Print Cookies

# Nutty Chocolate Crispy Cookies

*These biscuits are moreish and super crispy. They spread quite a bit when they are cooking so make sure you leave enough room between them. They also need to cool before removing from the tray, as they are fragile when warm.*

*Vegan | Gluten free*
*Makes 32*

50g butter, dairy or plant-based, softened
1/4 cup coconut oil
3 tablespoons Muscovado or brown sugar
1/2 can light condensed milk, coconut, oat or dairy
1 cup mixed nuts, pulsed until finely chopped
3 tablespoons desiccated coconut
2 tablespoons Dutch cocoa powder
3 tablespoons cornflour
4 tablespoons brown rice flour
1/2 tsp baking soda
125g dark chocolate, chopped into small chunks

Preheat the oven to 180°C. Line a tray with baking paper. Measure the butter, coconut oil and sugar into a mixing bowl. Using a paddle attachment or wooden spoon, mix well until pale. Add the condensed milk, nuts, coconut, cocoa, cornflour, brown rice flour, baking soda and chocolate. Mix until it just comes together – don't overmix.

Shape the biscuits into rounds using two teaspoons, one to scoop and the other to push off onto the tray. Try to keep them as round as possible and leave 3cm between each to spread.

Bake for 12–15 minutes. Leave on the tray for 5 minutes before transferring to a cooling rack to cool completely. Store in an airtight container, preferably a biscuit tin.

# Brown Sugar Shortbread

*Shortbread is a favourite in our house. Its buttery flavour and gentle texture is so satisfying and great to have at Christmas time, or any time really. They are the best tin filler as they have a long shelf life.*

## Vegan | Gluten free
## Makes 25 biscuits

225g butter, plant-based or dairy, softened
1/2 cup light muscovado or brown sugar
2 cups flour
1/3 cup cornflour or tapioca flour

### Gluten-free option
Replace flour with:
2 1/3 cups gluten-free flour mix
1/4 cup plant milk
1 tsp guar gum
pinch salt

Line a baking tray with baking paper. If making the gluten free version, you will need two pieces of baking paper to roll the dough between. Preheat the oven to 150°C. Measure the butter and sugar into a mixer or a large bowl and, using the paddle attachment of your mixer or a wooden spoon, cream the butter and sugar until pale. Add the flours and mix until it resembles breadcrumbs and is just starting to stick together.

Tip the dough out onto a floured bench (or on to baking paper for gluten free). Squeeze together and very lightly knead into smooth ball. Roll out into a 1cm thick x 5cm wide x 25cm length rectangle. Cut into 5mm pieces and place on the baking tray, cut-side down. Push or prick each one with a fork and bake in the oven for 30 minutes. Remove and cool slightly on the tray, then transfer to a cooling rack to cool completely. Store in a tin or airtight container.

# Peach Crumble Slice

*Everyone's favourite part of a crumble is the topping, right? There is still enough fruit on this upside-down crumble to balance it out – and baking the peaches on top caramelises them a little. The crumble layer is easiest to do in the food processor, otherwise just chop up the cashew nuts as small as you can and mix everything together in a bowl.*

*Vegan | Gluten free*

*Makes a 10 x 35cm slice tin*

1 1/2 cups cashew nuts
1/2 cup coconut oil, virgin or refined
1/2 cup coconut sugar
1 cup desiccated coconut
1 tsp vanilla extract
1 tsp baking powder
1 tablespoon cornflour or tapioca flour
1/4 cup coconut flour or brown rice flour
2 tablespoons runny honey, coconut nectar or brown rice syrup
10 peaches, apricots or nectarines, stone removed and quartered
1 tablespoon honey, coconut nectar or brown rice syrup

Grease a slice tin with a removable base and line the base. Preheat the oven to 180°C. Measure the cashew nuts, coconut oil, sugar, coconut, vanilla, baking powder, cornflour, coconut flour and first measure of honey into a food processor. Pulse together until the cashew nuts are chopped and the mixture is starting to stick together. Tip into the tin and push the base down evenly.

Arrange the quartered peaches on top of the crumble mixture and drizzle the second measure of honey over the top. Bake for 30 minutes.

Remove from the oven and cool in the tin. To remove, push the base up. You may need to loosen the edges a little first. Serve with yoghurt or cream or enjoy on its own.

# Fruity Frangipane Tart

In this tart you can really make use of seasonal fruits or use the macerated dried fruit option when your favourites are out of season.

## Vegan | Gluten free
### Makes a 28cm tart

### Pastry
100g butter, plant-based or dairy, softened
1/3 cup sugar
1 egg
1 1/3 cup flour
1/4 cup ground almonds

### Gluten-Free Vegan Pastry
100g plant-based butter
1 cup sorghum flour
1/4 cup pea or chickpea flour
1/4 cup cornflour, tapioca or potato flour
1/4 cup sugar
1/3 cup psyllium husk
2/3 cup hot water
2 tablespoons aquafaba

### Frangipane
1 1/2 cup walnuts or almonds, finely ground
200g butter, plant-based or dairy, softened
3/4 cup sugar
1 egg
2 tsp vanilla paste
1/4 cup flour

### Gluten-free Vegan Frangipane
Replace egg and flour with:
1 tablespoon ground flaxseed
1/3 cup cornflour

### Topping Options
12 fresh figs, quartered or 4 pears, peeled, cored and sliced into 5mm lengths
juice of 1 lemon
or
1 cup pitted prunes, figs or apricots soaked in 150ml marsala overnight

Grease a tart tin. Measure the butter and sugar into a mixing bowl and cream until pale. Add the egg, flour and ground almonds and mix to form a dough.

To make the Gluten-free Vegan Pastry, rub the butter into flours and sugar. Mix the psyllium and hot water together. Combine, then bring together with the aquafaba.

Tip out and kneed a little to bring together. Rest under the upturned bowl for 5 minutes.

Roll out to 3mm thickness and fit into the tin, pressing into all the ridges. Prick with a fork and use a sharp knife to trim the pastry from the edge of the tin, chill in the fridge for 10 minutes.

Preheat the oven to 180°C. Line the pastry with baking paper and fill with baking beads or beans and bake for 10 minutes. Remove from the oven. Remove the paper with the beads/beans and bake for a further 5 minutes. Remove from the oven and turn it down to 170°C.

Meanwhile, measure all the frangipane ingredients into a mixing bowl and, using the paddle attachment or a wooden spoon, mix until smooth. Transfer to the baked tart case and spread out evenly. Arrange the fruit on top of the frangipane. Bake for 45–55 minutes, until the frangipane is golden brown and risen. Cool for 5 minutes then remove from tin and cool on a wire rack. Serve with thick yoghurt, crème fraîche, custard or ice cream.

# Kumara Pie with Gingernut Crust

*A Kiwi take on a traditional American autumnal dessert. This kumara pie is smooth and velvety with warming spices and a sweet kick of ginger with a biscuity base. I used an orange/golden kumara but any variety will work just as well. I prefer a deep pie with plenty of filling to crust, but a thinner one is fine too.*

**Vegan | Gluten free**

**Makes a 20 x 4cm deep tin pie**

**Serves 9**

## Crust

1 cup wholemeal flour or 3/4 cup sorghum flour
1/4 cup cornflour
180g butter, plant-based or dairy, cubed and chilled
2 tablespoons coconut sugar or brown sugar
1 tablespoon golden syrup or malted brown rice syrup
1 egg (or 1 tablespoon ground flaxseed mixed with 2 tablespoons water)
1 tablespoon ground ginger
1/4 cup roughly chopped crystalised ginger
1/4 cup roughly chopped walnuts

## Filling

1kg kumara (2 cups of mash)
1 cup coconut cream
1/2 cup coconut sugar or brown sugar
4 tablespoons cornflour
1 tablespoon finely grated fresh ginger or 1 tsp ground ginger
1/2 tsp finely grated nutmeg
1 tsp ground cinnamon
a pinch of salt

## Topping

1 tsp ground cinnamon
1 tablespoon coconut sugar
1/2 cup chilled coconut cream, whipped with 1 tablespoon icing sugar
1/4 cup Maple Walnuts (page 83), roughly chopped
2 tablespoons crystallized ginger, sliced

Preheat the oven to 180°C. Prick the kumara and bake until soft, about 45 minutes (depending on the size). Remove from the oven and, when cool enough to handle, scoop out the flesh and mash well. You may need to put it into a food processor or push it through a sieve to remove the stringy bits.

Meanwhile, place all the crust ingredients in a food processor and pulse until combined. Grease a tart tin with a removable base. Tip the dough into the tin and, using wet hands, push it evenly on the base and up the sides. Chill in the fridge.

Preheat the oven to 170°C. Whisk the kumara purée in a bowl with the coconut cream, sugar, cornflour, ginger, nutmeg, cinnamon and salt. Pour into the chilled base, sprinkle the cinnamon and coconut sugar over the top and bake for 45–50 minutes for a thick pie or 30–35 minutes for a thinner one.

Remove from the oven and cool completely before removing the tin. Serve topped with whipped coconut cream and sprinkle with maple walnuts and crystalized ginger. Store covered in the tin in the fridge.

# UK - US Conversion Chart

## Spoons, Cups & Liquid

| Spoons & Cups | Millilitres |
|---|---|
| 1/4 tsp | 1.25 ml |
| 1/2 tsp | 2.5 ml |
| 1 tsp | 5 ml |
| 1 tbsp | 15 ml |
| 1/4 cup | 60 ml |
| 1/3 cup | 80 ml |
| 1/2 cup | 125 ml |
| 1 cup | 250 ml |

## Temperature

| Gas Mark | °C | °F |
|---|---|---|
| 1 | 140° | 275° |
| 2 | 150° | 300° |
| 3 | 170° | 325° |
| 4 | 180° | 350° |
| 5 | 190° | 375° |
| 6 | 200° | 400° |
| 7 | 220° | 425° |
| 8 | 230° | 450° |
| 9 | 240° | 475° |

## American Cups to Grams

| Ingredients | Grams |
|---|---|
| 1 cup butter | 225g |
| 1 stick butter | 113g |
| 1 cup flour | 125g |
| 1 cup white sugar | 225g |
| 1 cup brown sugar | 200g |
| 1 cup icing sugar | 125g |

| Ingredients | Grams |
|---|---|
| 1 cup raisins | 200g |
| 1 cup chia seeds | 150g |
| 1 cup syrup | 350g |
| 1 cup ground almonds | 110g |
| 1 cup rice (uncooked) | 200g |

# Index

A catalogue record for this book is available from the National Library of New Zealand.
ISBN 978-1-990003-91-2
An Upstart Press Book
Published in 2023 by Upstart Press Ltd
26 Greenpark Road, Penrose, Auckland 1061, New Zealand
Text and recipe photographs © Anna Valentine 2023
Photographs front cover & pages 6, 167, 240 © Ray Kreyl 2023
The moral right of the author has been asserted.
Design and format © Upstart Press Ltd 2023
Commissioning editor: Alison Brook
Editor: Jane Hingston
Cover, illustrations and text designed by Kathryn Swann
Printed by Dongguan P&C Printing Technology Co., Ltd.